Inspiring HOP.

Some VIP's comment about this book:

"Is the jar half full or half empty?" How many times does it look half empty? Hope for the future with a deep faith and belief in the future allows one to see it "half full"! I've been called the eternal optimist because I always see HOPE! My father used to say that God helps those that help themselves. The stories and experiences in this book prove that point. You will go away from this great read with hope for your future and the positive influence that you can have on others." **Jo Ann Bennett-Boltinghouse**

"Hope is the most powerful word in our language. No one ever achieved anything of significance without HOPE. Yet, sustaining hope can be difficult in challenging times, but that is when we need it most of all. This book is filled with inspiring stories that remind us that hope conquers fear, despair, and every problem in your world." -**Charles F. (Chic) Dambach, MBA**

"We joined Thom's marvelous project (see their story and chapter inside this book) because of his faith and commitment to helping people find **Hope** in a time when it is most needed around the world. The stories of these powerful speakers and writers can change your life in positive ways. This book is all about "keeping the faith; and living in hope more effectively! " **Drs. Charles & Elizabeth Schmitz**, Multiple Award Winning Authors, America's #1 Love/Marriage Experts, featured at TerrificSpeakers.com

"Hope is what the American Dream is built upon. This book will inspire and motivate you to 'turn adversity into advantage' and achieve Your Dream." –**Coach Rich Zvosec**

"How rewarding to be a part of hope. You will find stories, you will find teachings, and you will find the hearts of authorities in these pages. These writings not only look for hope but recognize it and embrace it, and inspire it within you. Hope is what keeps the world and people living, keeps you moving forward successfully. " **Liz Cosline**

"If 'hopelessness,' (according to psychiatrist Jerome Frank) is 'the inability to imagine a tolerable future,' then Inspiring HOPE is the design template and launching pad for escaping gravity and launching your mind-body-spirit into new realms of possibility and promise. Take 'hope' and take flight!" **Mark Gorkin, MSW, LICSW**

"It is very exciting to know that there is great wisdom being shared in this book! Hoping for the best and having an uplifting view of life is vital. People who make daily health deposits and invest in living at their best will continue to enjoy the fruit of their efforts through each season of life." **Angela Gracia Smith**

"What an inspirational read. Now is the perfect time in our history for these uplifting thoughts and terrific stories of Hope." **Dr. Susan Murphy,**

Your Feedback about this book is also appreciated! Please email us at ThomLisk@TerrificSpeakers.com

inspiring
HOPE

Dr. Thom A. Lisk

New York

ISBN 978-1-60037-640-5

Library of Congress Control Number: 2009904698

Cover Design by: Rachel Lopez rachel@r2cdesign.com
Cover Photo by Pulitzer Prize winning Photo Journalist Jerry Gay

MORGAN · JAMES
THE ENTREPRENEURIAL PUBLISHER

Morgan James Publishing, LLC
1225 Franklin Ave., STE 325
Garden City, NY 11530-1693
Toll Free 800-485-4943
www.MorganJamesPublishing.com

In an effort to support local communities, raise awareness and funds, Morgan James Publishing donates one percent of all book sales for the life of each book to Habitat for Humanity. Get involved today, visit **www.HelpHabitatForHumanity.org.**

Table of Contents or Menu of Hope

Introduction

On the same day, I spoke to two of my favorite people by phone, one based in California, and the other in Washington State. I am based in Ohio. Jerry Gay, award-winning photo-journalist, is based in the "upper left coast" area. The other person, Bill Driscoll, an ex-top gun pilot, and instructor of top-gun fighter pilots, gave me some wisdom for this book. "Going into combat without hope is risky business! You must have hope at all times in your life."

This book is uniquely useful starting with the front cover images and accompanying words, and story by story, photo by photo, contributor by contributor, **you will find great hope** for your life journey regardless of your age, gender, country of origin, etc. You will find hope to overcome every challenge, hope for a more successful tomorrow.

Each of us has a unique filter through which we see our reality; the better your hope-laced input the better your output or the better decisions you make moment by moment.

I was up before 6 am one day working on the material in this unique book because people desperately need more hope. One problem in writing is that it seems permanent... the spoken word does not seem quite as permanent as do written words or meaningful photos. You want **permanent improvement** in your life? You need to **live more hopefully each day**?! This book will help you day by day to gain more hope. You can draw closer to God and His eternal promises and principles; you will find more hope for your journey.

You may read one story from one of the contributors and love that story or chapter, yes, you identify with that—"great!". The next story you may think, "I don't now need this." Okay! There is **something for everyone in this book**, but not everything is for everyone right now. Keep reading!

Days come and go and so can hope if you do not cultivate and **keep hope alive**. The Top Gun pilot in combat either shoots the enemy down or is shot down. He hopes to fight another day. This book can help you to fight better each day, gain more victory due to more faith, hope and love.

More success for you in this life and the gift of eternal life through Ultimate Hope, these are my prayers for you as you embark on reading this book. Don't just read it, meditate on it, consider how to apply the story or success principles, and if you like a specific contributor help us, please, introduce that person to other people. Each of these contributors can be scheduled as an inspiring speaker by going to TerrificSpeakers.com where you phone or email.

As Pope John Paul 11 encourage the entire world in his Apostolic Letter, Novo Millennio Ineunte, **"Let us (always) go forward in hope!"**

I ASKED FOR STRENGTH

I asked God for strength, that I might achieve.

I asked for help that I might do greater things.

I was given infirmity that I might do better things.

I asked for riches, that I might be happy.

I was given poverty, that I might be wise.

I asked for power, that I might be praised.

I was given weakness, that I might be feel the need of God.

I asked for all things, that I might enjoy life.

I was given life, that I might enjoy all things.

I got nothing that I asked for, but everything I had HOPED for.

Almost despite myself, my unspoken prayers were answered.

I, among all, am most richly blessed.

When a time of crisis arises maybe overwhelming us in our lives, and more hope is needed, true hope, maybe we can read this prayerful reflection by an unknown confederate soldier penned during the USA Civil War.

Submitted hoping this helps you from Dr. Thom A. Lisk

(baby and senior.. seeing life from beginning to the end)

Contemporary wisdom is making breakthroughs in everyday understanding by revealing that we can only be responsible for the person we are at this moment. Our challenge is to stop and see who, what and where we are now without being influenced by our own negative thoughts or the necessity to impress others.

When we visualize each moment with positive perspectives, we summon the universal forces of life into our immediate reality. Within each moment, this affirmative vision begins to transform our very existence. Now we can see faith and hope everywhere to create a new world through our collective words and actions.

Jerry Gay, Pulitzer Prize Winning Photo Journalist

I Chose Hope—
and That Has Made All the Difference

Arlene R. Taylor, PhD

Most of the important things in the world have been accomplished by people who have kept on trying when there seemed to be no hope at all.
—Dale Carnegie

Yes indeed! I owe a great deal to teachers—two in particular. One of their names I recall. The other I only remember by my personal nickname for him. Most people are impacted by their teachers, negatively or positively. Fewer analyze and identify the impact. With some thought I was able to pinpoint how the influence of these two individuals changed the entire course of my life. Because of them I learned to hope. In fact, I may even be alive today because of them, because back then my life was not working. If being sick frequently with at least one bout of walking pneumonia annually, continual fatigue, experiencing my then-husband run off with my secretary, and feeling as if I could never succeed at anything, counted, then my life was not working. I had taken a new job, hoping it would be less stressful and a better fit with my aptitudes. So far, so good. Until my first performance evaluation at my new job as director of infection control at an acute hospital.

"It's time to start working on a Master's," my boss said, smiling encouragingly. I smiled back, but doubt that the smile reached my eyes. How could I explain that, as much as I loved to learn, getting a Master's degree was simply not in the cards? Not for me. I wasn't very smart. Besides, I would have to take statistics. And pass. And my brain didn't do math. My boss wouldn't let it go.

She kept bringing the topic up, and I kept making excuses. Enter Dr. Terrence Roberts, or "Doc T," as I thought of him.

In a serendipitous coincidence, my boss asked Doc T to provide some lectures, assessment, analysis, and personal feedback to nursing middle-management personnel. As a member of the faculty at a local 4-year college and director of Behavioral Health at our facility, he was eminently qualified to do so. At our first one-to-one meeting, he asked about the stressors in my life and what I planned to do, career-wise, with the rest of my life. I laughed and teared up as I repeated the pressure I felt to earn a Master's degree. I concluded by reiterating the fact that there was no hope of my ever accomplishing something like that. I was very lucky to be doing as well as I was (which, by the way, was not doing very well at all, but I didn't know the difference at that stage of my life—thinking that struggle, illness, and exhaustion was what adulthood was all about). He must have astutely seen through my convoluted thinking.

I have little recollection of anything he explained about my Johari-Window results. I do remember his posing half a dozen questions and suggesting I find time over the next few weeks to arrive at answers. Over time I've come to believe there are few accidents in life—just opportunities that we so often miss. Doc T was one of my great opportunities. Fortunately, I already held him in great professional regard, knowing that he had been one of the Little Rock Nine, one of a group of African-American students who had been enrolled in Little Rock Central High School in 1957. I figured that if he could survive that unspeakable hardship and abuse and go on to get a PhD, I could trust that he must know something. Maybe even something that could help *me*. After all, what did I have to lose?

I took his questions one by one and tried to answer them against the backdrop of my life experiences to date.

1. ***What made me think I was not smart?*** That one was easy. First, I'd always felt "different" from others. Second, when I made comments at the dinner table, family members frequently laughed. It had never occurred to me that I might actually have said something witty. And third, as I listened to people talk, my brain's perception of the topic often differed from theirs. These and a hundred other examples had come to be equated with *not smart*.

2. ***How did I know my brain didn't do math?*** That was one easy, too. At age 16, taking trigonometry by correspondence, I had actually equaled my age on the final-exam grade. 16%. My mother had been horrified. "When I was your age," she had said more than once, "I scored a perfect 100% on my trig final. How could I have a daughter who flunked? If you didn't look so much like your father and me I'd think the hospital had given us the wrong newborn..." And so it went between sighs and moans. That 16% coupled with my mother's bewilderment had translated into, *I'm math illiterate.* Since then I had accepted the fact that my brain just didn't do math. It could do other things: write verse and short stories, play and sight-read music, brainstorm new games, problem solve on the spur of the moment, glide around the ice rink...it didn't do math.

3. ***What stories had I heard over the years about my abilities?*** That one was harder. I had been home-schooled for nine of my K – 12 years. My internal explanation for being home schooled was that my parents thought I wouldn't be successful in a real school setting (although that had never been verbalized). I was the only student, and my "home school teacher" was a very high-IQ adult. A continual emphasis on missed test questions, versus no affirmation for

the ones I had gotten correct, contributed to a sense that "I couldn't do it right." There was also a big push for me to work on areas of weakness, rather than concentrating on what my brain did energy-efficiently. Current brain function rhetoric strongly suggests that such an antiquated view is not only unhelpful over the long term but also can contribute to multiple problems ranging from an increased risk of illness, to managing one's weight, to a potential decrease in longevity. But that information—in the era of brain imaging—was half-a-century away. So, concentrating on tasks that were difficult for my brain to accomplish led me to believe that my abilities were few and far between, and the ones I did have were not particularly admired or rewarded.

4. ***Did I know the stories I was telling myself about my abilities?*** No, not until Doc T suggested I identify them. They weren't pretty, those stories. They related primarily to fears of what I could NOT do successfully. Fears related to what others would think, of not fitting in, that my mother would die of breast cancer, that my father would not recover from "jaundice" (Hepatitis A), that I would forget the music for the piano recital (rote memorization being so difficult for my brain), and on and on. No wonder I was tired and sick and sick and tired. I had obviously accepted the mantra of fear as my own. That's a load for any brain to carry!

5. ***Had I grown up in an optimistic or pessimistic environment?*** I grappled with this question. Using the definition that optimism is a conclusion reached through a deliberate thought pattern that leads to a positive attitude, I had to conclude that my childhood environment veered toward the pessimistic side. For as far back as I could recall, the comments and instructions directed toward me had been couched in the negative: don't, can't, shouldn't, oughtn't,

won't, and so on. Much later in life I would be told by a brain-function specialist that although no family can truly be considered as functional, there are degrees of dysfunction. In a mildly dysfunctional family, estimates are that children hear nine or ten negatives for every positive. Double that for a moderately dysfunctional environment and triple it for an environment considered tobe outright dysfunctional. People tend to do what they have experienced, and you can only pass on what you know. Therefore, it's no wonder pessimism can be transmitted down the generational corridor.

6. *What had happened in my life to deprive me of hope?* That definitely set me back on my heels. Until then I didn't even realize I had none. According to Erik H. Erikson, the well-known developmental psychologist and psychoanalyst who postulated that a human being goes through eight stages from birth to death, hope is both the earliest and the most indispensable virtue inherent in the state of being alive. If life is to be sustained, hope must remain, even where confidence is wounded or trust impaired. Hopefulness is the clear sense that something I wished for might actually occur, that what I wanted might be possible. Somewhere during my childhood I had stopped wishing or wanting—just plodding along, one foot in front of the other, not thinking about anything I didn't already have. Double ouch!

It was several weeks before Doc T and I chatted about these six questions. It was even longer before I found the courage (at his suggestion) to take an IQ test. Part of me said it was better to wonder how non-smart I was—better than to have my beliefs confirmed. If Doc T hadn't kept encouraging me when our paths crossed in the cafeteria I might never had screwed up the courage. His premise was that my score would fall within the bell curve of distribution and that with a good teacher there was every reason to believe I could pass statistics. *Right.* The teacher could not be the issue. I hadn't had one. Not really. I had a correspondence course. My brain's inability to do math was the issue. That was *my story* and I stuck to it.

In retrospect, it is amazing how tenaciously we are wont to hang onto our stories and interpret everything that happens in their light. Eventually I returned to Doc T's office to learn the results. Eyes twinkling, Doc T told me that my score was definitely above 85—that being the lower end of the first deviation from the mean on the Bell Curve of Distribution. This removed all doubt (his words) about whether or not my brain could wrap itself around statistics. "The issue," he pointed out, "is whether you can alter your perception enough to risk taking a statistics course. I think you've given up hope." He was right. I had. But at his words the dim outline of a door marked *hope* began to materialize in my mind.

More time went by as I tried to picture my life differently, as I tried to rewrite parts of the script I had been handed at birth. Looking back, that represented a colossal waste of time, except that it gave me time to consider and reconsider the beliefs and attitudes I had consciously and subconsciously absorbed—many of them no doubt before the age of three. I was struggling to develop new habits of joy in an effort to change my mindset from pessimistic to optimistic. Once again this brilliant teacher came to my rescue. Drawing on a paper napkin he introduced me to Paul MacClean's *Triune Brain Model.*

Basically, think of the brain as three functional layers: two subconscious and one conscious. The brain thinks in pictures and deals easily with positives—a one-step process. What you see is what you get. The 3rd brain layer can process negatives, but it is a challenge—a two-step process, which involves the reverse of an idea. There's a huge difference between "Don't touch the stove," and "Keep your hands away from the stove." What you think in the conscious third layer filters down to the second and first layers and provides a map for them to follow. (The first and second layers can perceive language even though they don't use language per se.) And here's the rub. The first and second brain layers may be unable to process negatives at all. That's the reason affirmation is considered to be the programming language of the brain, the most effective way to communicate with the subconscious layers. It was a slow process to learn to recognize a thought as negative and figure out a way to state it as a positive. Slow, but possible!

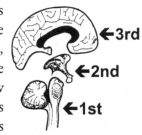

D-day arrived when Doc T tossed a college summer school bulletin across the table and casually remarked, "Go register for statistics. Keep it a secret, if you want to. When you pass you can enroll next fall in a Master's program."

"And if I don't?" I asked, half seriously and half in jest.

"Get a math tutor and retake the class." He was nothing if not direct. "Go ahead. Risk it."

Risk it? I looked up some information on risk. One person defined it as a function of three variables:

- probability that a threat exists
- probability that there are significant vulnerabilities
- potential impact of the vulnerabilities

If any of these three variables approaches zero, the overall risk approaches zero. My conclusions were that there was no real threat—only the possibility that I wouldn't make a "C," and someone else would find out about it. The only vulnerabilities were my abilities and my own perceptions. Hmm-m-m.

I signed up for summer school along with 58 other adult students. Believe me, I kept it a secret. The only people who knew, were my immediate family members (I would be in Statistics class four nights a week for the next six weeks and spending every available minute studying) and my best friend in San Francisco.

The Statistics instructor was male, middle-aged, bearded, and had a PhD in mathematics. *Wow! What a brain he must have!* Filled with apprehension, I slipped into a desk at the back of the room and did all those nervous little things I would have preferred to avoid: dropping my pen, knocking over my bottle of water, stuttering out my name when he reached my desk creating a roster.

"What is your reason for taking this class?" the instructor asked when he reached my desk. "You look like you're headed for the guillotine," he added. The class laughed. Blushing, I explained that my boss was pushing me to get a Master's degree, that statistics was a pre-requisite, and that my brain did not do math—unfortunate for me. Looking at me from the corner of one eye he calmly and deliberately tapped his pen on my desk. "Your brain will do math in my class," he said, matter-of-factly. The tiny crack appeared in the door marked *hope*. From then on I thought of him as Dr. H—H for hope.

Over the course of the next six weeks my brain worked beyond diligently. It over-learned, but I was still terrified that when push came to shove I might fail to pass. I doubt I've ever been as stressed in any other class before or since. I cannot even recall the instructor's actual name—just my nickname for him.

What I do recall in living color is how my brain felt in his presence. He believed that my brain could pass his statistics course, and I slowly absorbed some of his certainty. To my amazement, as the classes sped by, my brain not only seemed to "get it" at some level, but I also started to look forward to solving some of the statistical problems. Many of them involved aspects of epidemiology, an area of study that intrigued me. As each class morphed into the next, terms such as probability, reliability, mean, median, mode, and p-values actually took on some meaning. Gradually my apprehension lessened and my interest in the subject grew. Dr. H made it relevant. The crack in the door marked *hope* opened wider.

Each week there was a quiz. "Think of them," Dr. H explained, "as tools to tell you what you have already learned and what you still need to figure out." *What a concept!* "Your final exam will be your grade." *Oh, oh. Everything was riding on the final.*

One evening toward the end of class, Dr. H happened to be near my desk for one of his famous informal chats. He had a habit of wandering around the room and engaging us in conversation. His question to me was whether I knew what had triggered my math phobia. *Phobia? Did I have a phobia? Not me.* "So many bright women have one," he said, "and so often it is a figment of their imagination, albeit based on a real experience." My face must have mirrored puzzlement because he continued. "What they do is take one incident and build their self-concept around it."

In response to his question, I repeated my 16% final-exam story. When he found out that I had been taking trigonometry by correspondence he fairly howled with mirth. "That is simply rich," he roared, beard quivering as he went into peals of laughter. "You tried to teach yourself trigonometry and thought your brain did not do math. Oh, the stories we tell ourselves!" Somehow his laughter was infectious and soon we were all laughing as if it was the biggest joke in the world instead of the greatest tragedy in my math life to date.

"A student's success in math is a function of how well the teacher teaches," he said decisively when the laughter had died down. "And my brain's opinion (that phrase would become a life-time favorite) is that the overwhelming majority of individuals need a teacher. Trig by correspondence?" And he shook his head and started chuckling again.

Years later I would discover that study after study confirmed his opinion:

- Quality of the classroom teacher is the single most important factor in predicting student success.

- Teacher quality more heavily influences differences in student performance than does race, class, or school of the student.

- A teacher's knowledge of math matters for student learning in math at all school levels, but especially at the secondary level. Teachers who are more math-knowledgeable produce better student math achievement.

I chose to forego the annual 4th of July camping trip on the Mendocino coast. Oh, I went, but rather than lazy days of light reading on a chaise lounge listening to the music of the wind in the trees and the slap of water against the rocks, I studied. Statistics. Only the studying didn't seem the drudgery I had initially imagined. Images not only flashed onto the screen of my mind when I thought about the bell curve of distribution, probability formulas, and statistical significance, but the pictures made sense. During breaks from study I began to throw around possible topics for a Master's program. *Imagine! Dr. H had convinced me I could pass.* By the end of the camping trip I had my topics narrowed down to epidemiology and adult education—if I got a "C," of course. Hey, might as well go for a double major while I was at it!

The final exam was scheduled on the next to the last night of class. Dr. H would score the papers over the weekend and give out grades the following Monday. It was a timed test. As I did a quick scan of the exam I was surprised to note that the questions seemed familiar, and I was relieved that I knew the answers. If it had been almost any subject but math, I would have considered *passing* a done deal. All I needed was a solid "C" to get accepted to grad school. Finishing within the time frame, I turned in my paper and went home. To hope.

Monday night a large blank sheet of paper was taped to the blackboard. It was covering a list of students who achieved a grade of C or higher. When everyone was settled in their seats, Dr. H said he had enjoyed the last six weeks with us and expected we would be as successful in our next educational endeavor. He knew we could be. I heard virtually none of it. *Blah, blah, blah,* my brain thought. *Let's get to the scores and find out if he really knows what he has been talking about: that a student's success in math is a function of the teacher.*

Dr. H removed the paper. A list of names came into view, arranged in descending order of the number of points received out of a possible 500, along with the point spread for each letter grade. I looked for my name at the bottom of the list. *I only need a C! . . . Not there.*

My eyes moved up the list of C's. My name was not there. *That must mean I got a D,* I thought to myself. *How kind of him NOT to list my name, sparing me some humiliation.*

"YES!" The word exploded into the silence. It came from Yan, a young Chinese immigrant who was taking one evening class after another in his quest for a degree, while working full time to support a wife and daughter. "YES!" he shouted again.

Dr. H smiled and said, "Congratulations! You earned 500 out of a possible 500 points." We all clapped.

Turning to me, Dr. H continued, "And you, young lady, aren't you proud of yourself?"

"Yes," said Yan, "you gave me running for my dollars," meaning a run for my money.

My face must have mirrored my total confusion. "My name isn't on the board," I managed.

"Yes it is," they chorused in unison.

"Perhaps you didn't look high enough," Dr. H said, looking at me from the corner of one eye and moving his finger inexorably upward beside the list of names. Through the C's. Past the B's. Into the A's. *Into the A's?* Up, up, up until it stopped at the second name from the top. *At my name. It wasn't possible!*

Arlene Rose Taylor: 499 points—A+.

I had never exhibited behaviors even close to the *vapors,* but for a few moments I feared I would actually faint. *499 points? I'd missed a perfect score by 1 point?* My mouth gaped open in disbelief. *Unbelievable!*

In the moment of silence that followed, Yan patted my shoulder awkwardly and repeated a story he had heard in childhood. It seems, eons ago, a famine had struck a remote area of China. A father, seeing that he and his children would not live much longer since all their food was gone, filled some bags with ashes. Tying them with ropes from the ceiling, he told his little children, "There is roasted corn in those bags, but we have to save it for the future." Time passed and the father died of hunger. The children survived long enough to be rescued. They survived because they believed they had food. Their father died because he had lost hope.

"Your brain can do math, young lady," Dr. H said. "In fact, your brain can probably do most anything you need it to do—if you think it can."

In that instant, the course of my life altered. Passing statistics and enrolling in graduate school was the least of it. Dramatically, albeit slowly, my brain's perceptions changed. I came to understand the power of my own expectations to either limit or enable. And I experienced the power of another brain believing in mine, completely and unequivocally. Incontrovertible lessons.

A couple of earned PhD's and several published books later, I am convinced that no one is an island. In the words of John Donne, "Each is surrounded by a continent." These two teachers formed part of the continent around me. Their lessons positively impacted my life, as well, earning these teachers my undying gratitude. Oh, I know my brain did the work—no one could do the work for me. But I also know that Doc T and Dr. H exemplified the marine saying, *Ductus Exemplo* (leadership by example). They gave me hope and supported me to success.

Hope. The only blessing that remained in the Babrius jar, all that was left in Pandora's box.

Inspiring Hope! Waiting to be chosen, to be embraced.

Thanks to these two gifted teachers, I chose hope—and that has made all the difference. Christopher Reeve was right: "Once you choose hope, anything's possible."

From the Author Thom A. Lisk: I hope you enjoyed Dr. Taylor's story as much as I did! I hope you will become a Mr. or Ms. or Mrs. or Miss Hope to others everyday! You will love all the stories in ***Inspiring Hope!*** Some are much shorter stories, and some are longer and include more principles for your success! More copies of this book can be acquired by phoning in the USA 614-841-1776, or any of the contributors like Chic Dambach next, or Dr. Taylor.

Hoping for Peace; Building Peace

Charles F. (Chic) Dambach, MBA

Peace has been the hope of virtually every generation, culture, nation, and faith from the beginning of time. Yet, throughout history, ethnic groups, religious sects, tribes and nation states have wantonly resorted to violence – open warfare – to assert and impose their will. When my children study world history, they learn the story of war, and few believe it will ever change. The hope for peace is often dismissed as a superficial wish or the naïve chant of a counter-culture peacenik.

Violent force does not determine who is right, and the best ideas don't always win with guns and bombs. The only assured outcome of war is massive death and destruction. It is time for hope and wisdom, truth, and justice – the tools of peace – to prevail.

Building peace has become a powerful force supported by serious research, quality training of skilled conflict resolution specialists, and the development of institutions, systems and mechanisms to resolve differences without violence. As a direct result, the frequency and severity of violent conflict has declined dramatically. News headlines from the Middle East, Africa and South Asia create the impression that violence has consumed the planet, when in reality, peace is growing and violence is in decline.

15

The Global Peace Index, created by Australian philanthropist Steve Killelea, identifies dozens of countries all over the world that have become remarkably peaceful. Scandinavian countries, once the violent Vikings, now comprise the most peaceful region in the world. Vietnam, long engulfed in horrific violence, has become remarkably peaceful. Ghana and Madagascar have become beacons of hope for peace in Africa. Just a few decades ago, Chile was the scene of violent revolutions. Now, it is a model of peace and progress. **Peace is possible!** And, these nations are living proof.

Peace studies curricula are emerging in the best colleges and universities worldwide, including major military academies. These institutions help us understand the causes and the cures for war, and they are training violence prevention and conflict resolution experts. Peacebuilding professionals apply their skills and tools at all levels of society to help prevent and reduce violence. They are changing attitudes, and creating systems and mechanisms to facilitate dialogue, negotiation, and mediation. The concept of reconciliation is gaining ground over mindless and endless revenge and retribution.

Hundreds of peacebuilding organizations are emerging in the US and Europe, and they are growing out of the ashes of war in less developed countries. The West Africa Network for Peacebuilding based in Ghana is one of the best. The Foundation for Tolerance International in Kyrgyzstan is a remarkable counter point to violence in a volatile environment. Some organizations are faith-based and others are secular, but all work together to fulfill the same hope for peace. The Sant'Egidio peace program, formed by a religious order in Rome, has been a pioneer and model of success for four decades, while Rick Warren's Saddleback Church has recently made global peacebuilding a priority. The Institute for Multi-track Diplomacy was created by retired diplomat John McDonald, and former Finnish President Martti Ahtisaari created the Crisis Management Initiative, and he received the 2008 Nobel Peace Prize. The Alliance for Peacebuilding has 50 member organizations with expertise in violence prevention and applied conflict resolution, and the Global Partnership for the Prevention of Armed Conflict links peacebuilding organizations in each of 15 regions worldwide. Building peace is a new and growing global phenomenon, and it is *Inspiring Hope!*

Private Citizens are leading the way, but the UN and many national governments are vital components of the peacebuilding community. Together, we are designing and building a pathway to peace. I wish it could be a superhighway, but a walking path will do for now. *Inspiring Hope* and fortified by study, training, and hard work, people of goodwill, courage, and perseverance are building a more peaceful world for us all to enjoy.

(the humanity of all races)

The Teacher...The Cycle of Hope

Jo Ann Bennett-Boltinghouse

Her name was Miss Caulkins and she was beautiful, at least to me, a seven year old third grader on my first day in a new school. Miss Caulkins' world was a small, white country schoolhouse in Nance County, Nebraska. What I didn't know then, that I now know, is that I was on the threshold of my career for life. I was being handed over to "a perfect woman, nobly planned." I would be putty in the hands of a master. She would influence my life profoundly and she and I were not aware that she was sculpting a future teacher. Teachers play such an important role in molding the future of the leaders of our country; the butchers, the bakers, the fancy dressmakers; the moms, the dads and soldiers of the next generation. Teachers instill hope and introduce the possible. Our life is molded by choices, some of those we make ourselves, and others over which we have no input.

This brings hope for the future. Through no fault or action of our own we can be put in a place that leads us to other life changing choices. We need _Inspiring Hope!_

And so it was spring of 1944 that a really big change occurred in my life. My father had moved us away from my security of the "home place" to the unknown 125 miles down the road. Before that March I had lived in the same house, had the same friends, and gone to the same country school. I was shy and fearful and definitely did not want to go to a new school. Fear of the

19

unknown has been found to be one of the strongest fears. It can keep us from moving forward towards goals and adventures. All I knew then was I was not feeling comfortable with my parents' insistence that I go to a strange new school.

My parents and I finally arrived at a solution. Dad promised he would always take me to school and pick me up. After all, it was two miles each way (and uphill both ways as my kids now say). Dad would take me on the tractor and then he would continue to a near-by farm to do his daily work in the fields. In the winter he added chains to the tires to get through the drifts that the road crew had not yet cleared. He kept his promise and I learned how important it is to keep your word. I learned what it feels like to have someone keep their word and know you are safe in the promise. It is a lesson I learned well, and one I live by to this day. "Under promise and over perform or a promise made is a promise kept."

The first day at the new school arrived. I was seated a front row seat because of my height. I was in the third grade; the only one in third grade. I felt so alone. Everyone knew each other, and I was the outsider. I was sure I would never have any friends. I dreaded recess because I knew no one would want to play with me. The school had no indoor plumbing and a trip to the "outhouse" was unthinkable. Everything about this "new" school was frightening.

Miss. Caulkins must have had a degree in psychology as she seemed to know just how I felt. She made me feel welcome and made sure I had someone to play with at recess. I know now that she was a thoughtful and wonderfully kind teacher. She became and has remained my favorite teacher.

After several weeks she suggested that my Dad not pick me up after school. I could ride home with her in her gray '39 Plymouth as she drove right by our driveway on her way to her home in Brunswick. That after-school time and the ride home became a very special time for me. I helped her wash the blackboards, check papers, make copies on the purple hex graph (does that date me!), dust shelves and stack books. She made me feel as though I was really helping her and that made me feel worthwhile and important. I liked those feelings and they gave me hope that the new school could turn out to be pretty neat after all. I began thinking I wanted to become a teacher, "just like Miss Caulkins."

My favorite game to play growing-up was to "play school." My dolls were the best educated in all of Nance County! I even dressed my cats and had them as students. I made lesson plans, learned poems for my dolls, and performed plays for my parents and friends. I was always the teacher in these performances.

Elementary and High School flew by. I had set my goal early on in school to go to college and become a teacher. High School graduation was just around the corner and the truth of my situation sat heavy on my heart; my parents were not financially able to send me to college. Undeterred at the ripe age of 16, I would get a job and save, save, save. But, by the grace of God, angels came to my rescue.

Always active in my church and attending church camp every summer, I made friends with several ministers and professors at the college campus where church camp was held. The summer after graduation one of those college professors and a local minister found out I was not planning to attend college. They immediately helped me apply for a Methodist Scholarship. I received as a full ride scholarship eliminating my parents' financial concerns. I enrolled at Simpson College In Indianola, Iowa and I felt I was truly in heaven. I loved the college atmosphere and the studying. I had begun my journey to become the teacher I had always wanted to be. I read everything about teaching, built a large children's literature file and was enraptured with student teaching.

Teaching was all I had thought it would be. My first year I had thirty-seven students and, just like Miss Caulkins, I taught third grade. The classroom was in a converted basement room at the Avenue B School in Council Bluffs, Iowa. There were no Teacher Aids or Special Education Teachers in our building. I was with those thirty-seven children all day, every day and I loved every minute of it. Hope for the future of my students was snowballing into a full blown mission statement. I was going to do everything humanly possible to see that they were set on the path to exploring possibilities. I would challenge their fears; then have them meet with success. I'd provide an environment where a positive self-image could flourish. I exercised my passion for reading when I introduced quiet time on the "reading rug". Each day, after lunch, the children would form a circle on the large braided run and I would read a book to them. At the beginning it was a short story from a new book. By November, I was reading a chapter a day from a library book. The children loved it. As an incentive when they finished their work, they could take a book and go quietly to the "reading rug".

Each year brought me new and exciting children. Each year there were two or three that stood out as outstanding students and equally two or three students who would require special attention needing more ***Inspiring Hope!***

I would like to introduce three students to you. Their stories illustrate the role teachers' play in the nurturing of the future hope for America. A teacher spends more "awake" time with their students during those formative years than do some parents. I hope these stories will bring back pleasant memories of a teacher who instilled hope in your dreams and pushed you to become all you could be. You can be that person for others!

We'll call our first student Marvin. Marvin had trouble learning and had repeated kindergarten, first grade, second grade and now at age eleven he was in my third grade class. Marvin was not eligible for any special education program because he had three siblings already in special programs and the school system felt that was too many from one family. So Marvin had to be "blended" into a regular classroom.

I can't even imagine how frustrated he must have felt. Marvin was bigger than everyone else and definitely more physically developed. He liked to walk under the open stairway when the girls went upstairs. My challenge was what to do with Marvin, how to teach him skills, and how to not have him disrupt the rest of the class. I shifted my mission statement into overdrive. Marvin's needs were going to be met and the third graders and I were about to provide an environment in which it could happen. Each day someone went into the little "back room" off our room and read a story to Marvin. Everyone helped him practice writing his name, and he learned to write his numbers to fifteen. Marvin restacked the books, cleaned the cupboards, and sorted papers. I had the cleanest, neatest cupboards and shelves in the building. Marvin was proud to be a contributing member of the classroom and there was no doubt that he qualified to be closet organizer by the end of the school year. He was proud of his well earned skill. He felt loved and a part of the class. It was the best gift I could give him. I often wonder what happened to Marvin. I have tried to find out through searches on the internet but have met with no success. Marvin seems to be off the radar. Wherever he is, I hope he is happy and working up to his abilities. Maybe he is *Inspiring Hope* somewhere.

I left teaching to raise my family and returned to the classroom when my youngest entered kindergarten. I was asked to move from the third to the first grade classroom. I was apprehensive about the move. Could I teach children to read? First graders were still so young and I was used to children who could write, work on their own and were somewhat independent. I accepted the challenge and I never looked back. It was a joy to teach children to read! To see their eyes as they put letters together to make words and, then words together to make sentences. It never ceased to awe them and me. I had truly found my niche.

One of my first graders has been a real inspiration to me. Her name is Robin and I have followed her personal life and career. She was a bright little girl that lit up the room with her enthusiasm and zest for learning. That year I was able to do a pilot reading program and Robin excelled. Each day I met with each individually. Their daily work of reading, math, and spelling was designed around their level of reading ability. There were no reading groups and every student had the opportunity to excel at their own reading speed and proficiency. Robin just zoomed through the books. By April, she was reading on the fifth grade level. Robin now uses her proficient skills as the office manager of a successful dental clinic. She is a reading model for her three sons. She recently told me that one of the things she remembers, after all these years, is the "reading rug". And so, the cycle of hope and possibilities inspired by a teacher continues.

My philosophy has always been that children learn by doing, so many of the units I developed were around classroom activities and field trips. Each year we made a Christmas Cookbook for their mothers. Out came the math unit using measuring spoons and measuring cups. The world of seconds and minutes erupted in a cacophony of egg timers. With recipes in hand, we'd head to the school kitchen to test our culinary skills on "choice" recipes, like Nana's extra chocolate, chocolate cookies, Aunt Lureen's

Swedish Cookies, and Mrs. Boltinghouse's Pop Corn Balls. A lesson on table manners concluded with eating our creations . The cookbook cover would be adorned with the collective smiling faces of the children. The lesson was always well received and I've since learned that several of those aspiring cooks still have those cookbooks. Robin recently shared hers with me so I could photo-copy it.

I believe these activities are fundamental to learning so I continued to expose them to new learning situations. The children were again involved in a "hands on" activity with yearly spring trip to the farm. Not only did they see and touch the baby animals but they brought back cream to churn into butter and made baking biscuits to spread it on.

Spring also meant it was time to prepare for the Mother's Day Tea. The class wrote their own poems and their own play. They again prepared the food. It was enlightening to the Mom's to see their children exhibit so much talent. They were very proud Moms. I have former students who remind of those activities. Some can even remember the lines they spoke in the play, the songs they sung, and how the room was decorated.

Do we realize the impact that learning has on students; the life skills they are going to take with them into adulthood? Being a role model for children is so powerful. The potential for good and bad is enormous.

One day I was getting my drivers' license renewed when a young woman came up to me and said, "You might not remember me, my name is Lisa and you were my first grade teacher." My memory flashed back to a curious little girl of six. There she was, Lisa, who reminded me so much of myself at her age. She, like me, had come from a meager background but was lit by the light of learning. Lisa had always been an eager student and a willing participant in the classroom. She went on to introduce me to her daughter and her baby granddaughter. Wow! Does that make one feel old! Apparently, Lisa had a baby shortly after graduating, as had her daughter. Lisa shared a little of her life. It was a pleasant encounter but it was soon folded in with my many other memories.

Three years later in a local restaurant our paths crossed again when Lisa was our waitress. She talked about how quickly her grandchild was growing up. I had just published my first children's book and so I asked her if I could give her an autographed copy for herself. I signed it and gave it to her with a special note inside. She later came up to me with tears in her eyes and thanked me for the impact I had on her life.

Well, the story doesn't end there. A year or so later, Lisa was still working in the same restaurant and again came to take my order. She told me that she had applied for a job at the school and was excited about the possibilities. I congratulated her, and asked if it was for a position as an aid? She said, "Oh, no, I applied for a teaching position. I have been going to school nights, and summers for ten years and I have my teaching degree!" How proud I was for her.

Lisa's story continues, as she is now a teacher and Shelby Center Supervisor of the Head Start Program. Lisa is a very productive member of the community and making a significant impact on many young lives. The cycle continues, from Miss Caulkins to Mrs. Boltinghouse to Lisa. It is a never ending cycle of hope, of encouragement. It is the continuation of my mission to teach, mentor and become a role model for children. Teachers are truly building a bridge of hope for children. We live in a troubled, confused world, and children and young adults are exposed to many situations that would never have entered our minds. The world is changing and teachers are the "hope of the future!" My mission still is "to help each person be the best at what they do and who they are, no matter what that is!"

How many adults are succeeding in life today because of a teacher that was an important role model in their lives; a teacher who made time to be available? Teachers are able to change the world one child at a time. I can smile with contentment when I think about Marvin, Robin, and Lisa. You too many have had, perhaps unknowingly, an impact on the lives of people. I am sure there are many who will never have the opportunity to thank you. Just remember, "The words you say to a child today will remain with them for a lifetime!"

Thank you Miss Caulkins for instilling and *Inspiring Hope* in me and opening the door to a world of possibilities. It is my continued hope that the legacy of learning forever burns brightly inspiring more and more hope and results.

Stepping Into the Unknown

Greg Bennick

Sometimes we need to search for hope in the midst of what feels like hell. The mind is powerful beyond words in terms of its control over how we feel about the situations we encounter. It has the ability to turn a situation that could hold the promises of heaven into something which feels impossible and dark and impenetrable. And the tricky part is that we often don't realize that this has happened until we have already trapped ourselves in the mire with seemingly no way out. But we get to decide which experiences are our heavens, and which are our hell.

If we keep our eyes open as we go through life, we can find metaphors for the entanglements that we are facing. Reflect on your recent experiences and you might find examples of exactly what I am referring to. I found one just yesterday. I was in Canada at a park called Whytecliff Park in West Vancouver. It's a heavily wooded area along the shore, gorgeous in that way that only British Columbia has to offer with tall evergreen trees, cool air, and a sense of the unexplored. This particular park has a twisting path that leads down a sharp hill to a small beach. At the end of that beach, there is a line of rocks and boulders about five feet wide jutting out of the water, stretching perpendicular from the shoreline. The path extends maybe four hundred feet out from land to an island the size of a city block on which you can climb and sit to watch seals, eagles and nature in all its glory laid out in front of you. I wanted to go out there to reflect and just breathe. To access the island, you have to step carefully from rock to rock as you make your way from land through the water, to the island itself.

I got to the island and climbed up the steep bank on its shore. I walked over and across it, to a point at the end where, while sitting with my back to the rest of the island with the original shore even further behind, I felt like I was at the end of the world. It was so calming. I spent two hours there and found all the answers I was looking for. I typed them all into a file on my laptop to return to later and exalt in the clarity that fresh air and calm moments had provided. I thought about how people can work together more effectively, why we struggle, why we fight, how we can communicate in deeper ways in our work place and in our lives with those we encounter every day. I wrote for two hours. And then I decided to head back.

As I walked back across the island I was immediately frozen in horror. I looked for the pathway and saw that the tide had come in. The path back to shore was no longer there, and in its place were only waves and the flowing icy cold tides over where the path had been. My mind raced. "What can I do? Who can I call? Can I sleep on this island overnight? It's too cold. Can I find shelter? Can I scream for help? I can't get back to shore." I had a hundred thoughts in the span of three seconds. I could feel my heart pumping hard in my chest. My mind went blank. I am stranded on an island with no one to help me. My mind raced as I walked closer to the edge of the water. I stood trying to figure out what to do.

And suddenly, I did something that came to me without thinking. It came clearly, without thought, without planning, without expectation or analysis. I had no other choice, and I wasn't even choosing. My left foot stretched out before me and I walked into the water.

The water was freezing. The second it hit my skin it felt like my body temperature suddenly dropped to zero. The first stone was close. I put my foot out to it and sank up to my knee. I expected to slip and fall. But the foothold was sound. I took my second step. A little deeper, but the same thing. As I walked, I realized that sometimes my depth perception was off and I could barely see the bottom, yet the stone I was looking for was right underfoot. Other times, I was sure of my footing, and as I put my foot on what I thought to be just the right place, I fell in all the way up to my waist. As I walked, carefully, step by step, the pounding heart subsided. It transformed into something else. It shifted into lightheartedness and laughter. I must have made a funny sight. Laptop held high above my head, soaking wet against unbearably cold tides, laughing out loud and loving every second of it.

As I walked through fear and into the experience, I realized that I was going to be fine. Yes, I would be soaking wet and freezing cold. Yes, I would have to buy new shoes or at least dry them for a year. But I realized that not only was I going to be okay, but that I would have an amazing story to tell of the experience. The thing is, my mind would have stopped me but my heart led me forward. I felt the experience, I submitted to it, and then let my mind catch up later. For that flash of a moment, I had been ready to stay on that island. Was it emotional intelligence that let me know that I would be okay? Was it self awareness that led me to know that I have good balance and wouldn't slip? Or was it just a determined courageous drive that let me take that first step into the water? Maybe it was a combination of all of those.

Process feels like that sometimes. You don't know where you are. You have no idea how to get to where you want to be. You feel trapped, scared, and alone. It's like being at the end of a tunnel and looking for light. Sometimes there is light at the end of the tunnel and you walk towards it. But other times, the tunnel offers only the unforgiving dark. In those moments, like my walk from the island, if you want to find out what getting to the end of that tunnel feels like, the only thing you can do is close your eyes, open yourself to experience, and take that first step into the dark.

What islands do you find yourself stranded on throughout your day? Is it the loss of a dream? Is it the fear of the unknown? I see islands all around me today. And I see myself standing on them. Will I have the courage to step off from a situation which feels truly awful and into the unknown in order to get to the place I need to be? I hope I do. And I hope you do too. Ultimately, my story isn't even the story of hope I am writing about. The story of hope I truly want to read, and the one which belongs in this book, is the one you live as a result of reading these words. I hope sincerely that you get in touch to share your story with me of how you took your first step into the unknown and walked off your island, and also what it felt like when you made it safely back to shore.

Note from Author Thom A. Lisk: This wonderful contributor, and all others, have their contact info in the back of the book; or you can find them at TerrificSpeakers.com You will love all the stories that follow, please keep reading! The ten photos (next is the third) tell a sequential story too!

(peace is at the end of the road)

Stolen Hope Regained!

Helene B. Leonetti, MD

I looked up into the eyes of the psychiatrist as she said, "How do you feel?" How do I feel----feel? "What do you mean, how do I feel?" I was supposed to die.

Mothers Day 1990 was bleak and overcast. Being a physician, I had easy access to the medicine closet in out office that stored the drug samples provided happily by the pharmaceutical reps. Ambien was then a big seller, as insomnia is a common issue, especially for menopausal women, and the box of 100 pills seemed a good choice.

I often reflect on my despair: I remember trying to think of one person to call that could discourage me from ending my life, but sadly I could not.

Looking out the window that May 13th, seeing the beautiful, lush gardens and the birds playfully splashing in their bath, I remember also feeling not joy nor comfort.

Why would someone so loved, so accomplished, so regularly happy and optimistic want to die? I badly needed hope!

For twenty years, I had practiced nursing and loved being a caretaker. But I also struggled with the medical profession with its pedantic, authoritative approach to patient care. At age thirty six, divorced from my son's father, I was catalyzed into medical school, figuring that if I did not approve of how my patients were being treated, I needed to do it myself.

Being told repeatedly that I was too old and my B average was not good enough to train in the United States, I went to Mexico where, becoming tan, perfecting my Spanish, and living with a Mexican family, I merged into the Latin culture.

Finally, in my forties, I arrived, finishing my residency in obstetrics and gynecology. My chairman, finding my vulnerability as I mourned the sudden death of my beloved second husband, wined and dined me into marrying him, a near fatal decision.

That ballsy, free-spirited, fun-loving me, succumbed into a tormented shadow of my former self because I gave this man my power, my individuality, my very soul---a grave misjudgment that would catapult me into a life-threatening depression.

You see, while my happy face was saying yes, my soul was screaming <u>NO</u>. This schism spiraled me into such depths that my joy for life slid away, moment by moment. The soul has a way of squeezing the heart into action. We cannot continue the illusion of peace and harmony when our world is being torn inside out.

Combine that with a teenage son who was spinning my buttons, knowing this man was not good for me; consider that I was an obeisant nurse transforming into the all-knowing authority figure of a doctor; and finally, witness the physical/emotional out-of-body experience thrust upon me by menopause: my suicide was easy to understand.

Fast forward almost two decades: healed from the pain, out of this destructive relationship, I now have a wonderful practice where I teach women how to love and honor themselves. Yes,

I am still a gynecologist, although I lovingly refer to myself as a 'recovering doctor.'

I specialize in the menopause, combining my training as an herbalist and expertise using human-identical hormones with nutritional and self-loving counseling. I always say that God gives women menopause to force us into self-love.

It is neither unique, nor original to say that all our spiritual teachers speak of the following as essential for having a joyful and peaceful life:

- Forgiveness
- Compassion
- Unconditional Love

What is best to be stressed is that we need to practice these on self before others. We as women particularly are so toxic, so very unkind in our thoughts to ourselves. Our niggling ego is constantly prattling:

- "I am too fat"
- "I am not smart enough"
- "I have no time for me, my children, my spouse, parents, etc., need me"
- Look at my cellulite, my spider veins, my sagging breasts"

As Pema Chodron, the Buddhist nun says: "Exercise limitless friendliness and compassion for yourself." In fact, unadorned and as you were born, stand in front of the mirror, look into the mirror of the soul—the eyes—and state: "I love you exactly as you are." Then watch the magic. Give yourself *Inspiring Hope!*

That life threatening experience was a sentinel moment in my soul's journey. I had to lose myself to rise up again from the ashes of self-hatred to one of self-love.

Today, each of my beautiful patients receives a hug as she leaves the office. Although they come for their Pap smear and breast exam, they receive so much more: a reminder that each of us is a perfect child of God who must love herself first—after God—before trying to care for others.

You know, we always teach most what we need to learn. My need to achieve great heights and be better and better was spurred on by my lack of self esteem. Finally, shortly before my sixty-fifth birthday, I awoke, and said to myself: "Helene, you are enough!" We mothers martyrs (as I call us all) must give way to the secure, self-loving women who are role models and serve to change our world. We have no time to play small.

And because our birthright is perfect health when we follow the principles of God's teachings---I remind my precious women—so magnificently stated by the quintessential physician, Albert Schweitzer that "the doctor is sent to entertain the patient while God does the healing."

Hopeful Thinking!©

Dr. Thom A. Lisk

Hope is not wishful thinking… it is much more. Because of prior conditioning of my thinking, I think of True Hope as a great certainty. How are you conditioned?

Now, none of us fully knows the future, but I have confidence that God will continue to hold the future as He has held the past together so as to bless me so I can bless you. This is an important hope. But there is much more!

Because God loves you and wants to bless you, He wants you to be hopeful. God by His Spirit creates hope within us. I can manifest that hope outwardly or hoard it inside—it is obvious as to which is best. Manifest hope to others and you will have better relationships, and many other better things in your life—that has been my validated experience.

Yes, God loves you and wants to give you a life of great and empowering hope. And, whether you are a deep and/or big believer in God or not you must have experienced at some point in your life the super great value of inspired hope.

Christmas Eve is the day I write this, what a hopeful day for millions, if not billions of people all over the world. Consider please that if everyday was Christmas Eve Day in your life— that is you lived as if tomorrow you were going to give and receive some very wonderful hoped for gifts—would you live your life any differently?

Would you move with more of a bounce in your steps, more grins on your face if today was the day before some great anticipated blessing coming into you life? Yes you would!

Well… live today—and everyday—as if tomorrow is going to be such a great and glorious day and today—and everyday—will be an excitingly hopeful day—life will be fantastic! You will be the kind of person that people love to be around. You will attract more positive people and things too.

It occurs to me that here I must mention that there seems to be different kinds of hope. And, I do not want you to simply become hopeful for "more things" in your life. It is the intangible blessings of life that are often the best.

Today my wife and I serve as both Lectors and Eucharistic Ministers at our Catholic Church's 4pm Christmas Eve service before going to one of our five married children's homes for dinner and Christmas Cheer and an exchange of gifts. I have a great anticipation for what the balance of today will unfold. I am not just thinking about tomorrow, I need today to be wonderful, and so do you every today of your life need today to be super terrific! Think about it.

During a Catholic Mass—take my word for it if you are not Catholic—uncountable blessings are dispersed whether you are ready to receive them or not. However, the Church teaches what my experience confirms—**prepare yourself** for the Words and images and all else that flows from the Mass Service and you do receive more. It starts with a general absolution of all venial sins… what a great start! We are asked to recall our sins and ask for God's holy pardon, and the priest who is empowered, prays for us all.

Now I will not go into a line by line explanation of what happens during a Catholic Mass or other Christian Church Services but truly the blessings are out of this world! A major point to be made is that if I did not come into the experience with hope, I may not leave the building full of hope. And, the best things hoped for are very intangible, like the forgiveness of sins. My soul is cleansed so that I can live a life of service more pleasing to God and more beneficial to His children, that is **people like you.**

Possibly the greatest and/or most dramatic turn around I have ever experienced in my life from a life of despair to a life of great hope has come as a result of going to what is commonly called "confession" in the Catholic Church.

This act of "confession" is a very Biblical thing to do, regardless of what some might assert, and it is one of the seven Sacraments of Holy "Mother" Church. Now lest I go to preaching, please realize I am here witnessing to my experiences (while working to bring Inspiring Hope!) about how I regained lost hope. So can you! Story:

One workday I was feeling that God had nearly abandoned me, or maybe it was a lack of motivation to work at my best with the right attitudes—this is how most would describe the feeling I was having. What do you do at a time like that? In my case I examined my conscience and realized I had some un-confessed sins bothering me. They fell into the category of the BIG seven mortal or deadly sins the church says we need to go to the Sacrament of Reconciliation (confession) for—in other words confess them to a priest for absolution. So, I drove about 15 miles at the noon hour to a Catholic Church that offers a priest after an 11:45—12:15 p.m. daily Mass. It was the best one hour investment of time I could make—20 minute drive, 20 minutes at the Church, 20 minute drive back to my office—as that afternoon my hope and positive expectant attitude returned and the balance of the day was happy and productive. By the way, the Catholic Church bases their confessional on teachings right from Jesus as recording in the last few verses of John's Gospel, chapter 20, you can check it out.

It was like a miracle! Yes, I experienced a miracle of God's mercy and grace. And, I have experienced that kind of miracle many times in my life, thanks to our loving and forgiving merciful God. Whatever you do, wherever you live or work, you need a clear conscience to live in HIGH HOPE.

From this point on in this chapter, I think I must now tell you some more very important things.

The Authors of the best kinds of hope are not the authors of this book, all the well intentioned people who all make great contributions. The Author who makes all of life worthwhile, and this book worthwhile too, is our God.

If this book finds its way to you, it is because it has been undergirded throughout the writing and publishing process with lots of prayer. The book is now dedicated in writing to God the Father, God the Son—Jesus, and God—the Holy Spirit. If you don't like some aspect of this book, take it up with our God. Whether you are a triune Christian or not, realize that God wants to offer you Inspiring Hope!

Now, I can not fully endorse each line from each co-author unless what is written is in full alignment with my understanding of what God would endorse. But, this does not mean that I will edit what others write out of this book, even though I (Thom A. Lisk) am the one responsible for seeing the book published and am called the "author". We all have our first amendment rights in America—**we must believe in freedom of speech.** (That is not the same as a free speech although we may be willing to give one to non-profit or church groups, just call or email us and ask.)

I would prefer to be paid for my speech or speeches or seminars, just like the people who write chapters in this book likewise who want to and need to be paid. However, I also give FREE speeches for groups including at Churches, Rotary Clubs…you name it. I and the other speakers featured herein <u>know how to edit and customize our speeches</u> so as to inspire audiences while never offending. Please invite us!

I would not speak to a business audience for pay as I have over 1000 times like I would to a Church audience. If I were to talk to a business audience or college audience or a group of top sales people for a Fortune 500 corporation, I could talk about **hoped for business**: how to stay motivated, plan properly for it to come about, and execute towards the important goals in a hopeful way.

> Everyone needs hope at all times! Hope is like the fuel that drives your engine, the best gas for your journey.

Again, today is Christmas Eve Day. The stock market closed the day on the upside, barely, after some dark days that brought the **Dow Jones Industrial** Average from over 14,000 to under 8000 in one year, and then slightly back up again closing today early at 1 p.m. due to the holiday on 12/24/08 at 8,468.48. You may have been one of the people that have lost thousands in the stock market decline. You need hope for the future! (It got much worse in 2009 before turning around starting the second week of March.)

Today on the business channel CNBC predicted the year ahead would be "bleak for investors". The bears seem to be drowning out the voices of the bulls. However one hopeful voice today on TV pointed out some stocks that were now or very soon extremely good buys and would increase double or triple in the months ahead. <u>You can always find hope.</u> Even if the markets go down or sideways hopeful people do their homework and **make money even in a worldwide recession.**

Why invest if you are not hopeful for some kind of return?

We invest in a variety of ways each day of our lives, it may not be the stock market it might be investing in the lives of your children or grandchildren, not with gifts that take money, but you invest time—a commodity far more important than money. I have lost money and know I can regain it by investing or spending more wisely next time, but I can never regain a moment of precious time. You invest your time wanting a return at your work, and you can **invest time to deposit hope into the lives of others.**

You can not give something you do not have to give. We must remember this truth. And, it is better to <u>give now</u> rather than wait until tomorrow. Who can tell for sure if we will be alive to give tomorrow!? **Do it now!—this is always a great motto. And do it now due to *Inspiring HOPE!***

Thinking about giving is not enough, is it?! You give most often out of sense of hope. You give thinking you are making a difference. Sometimes I give just because it is the right thing to do.

These last lines caused me to get one of my checkbooks out and write a check so that I will be ready to give during the Church Service I alluded to earlier in this chapter. I am prepared better now, in a sense of hope. God is more pleased with me if I come bearing some predetermined gift.

Is it any different elsewhere in our lives day in and day out? Come prepared to give! **Give people inspiring hope!**

Honestly my research and experience bears out the assertion that it is always more blessed to give than receive. If a person gets up in the morning with a grateful heart and attitude ready to give all day long—not living to get but rather to give—life goes along much better.

Sometimes we must prepare ourselves so we can give more.

Take a few steps back first. Maybe you need to go back to college, as one example, so as to open new doors in the future that will bring you more income. Life is Terrific!!!

Life begins today!!!—at whatever age you find yourself. We had a 90th birthday party for my award-winning retired school teacher mother recently, so I plan to be productive to at least age 90, by God's grace, and maybe to age 105 like my maternal grandmother who was married 73 years to my wonderfully beloved grandfather.

Yes!—hope is much more than just wishful thinking. You must **act upon your hopes to make your hopes and dreams come true**, whatever those might be! Keep reading to clarify your hopes and dreams into goals.

Next Christmas will be here—or the next New Year—before you know it so do not delay! Make every minute count with hopeful action regardless of the economy around you. Yes, be careful, be wise, get more good advice, but do something to **prepare for a brighter day ahead.**

When it is all said and done… you can't take anything with you beyond the grave. What you give will determine your legacy. Give even if it seems to hurt. Give even if you can't seem to find much to give. You always have something to give. You can give an electronic thank you or Christmas cards, but **don't delay**.

It need not cost you much or any money to hopefully create a brighter future.

Stop using and looking for excuses!

Randy Snow, a super great speaker friend, winner of Gold in the Para-Olympics, gave me a black T-shirt that hangs in my closet to see everyday—it reads, "What is your excuse?!" Randy has been in a wheelchair most of his adult life, yet he lives one of the most exciting and productive (and profitable) lives. In my office I have a poster autographed from Randy with a picture of him exulting in victory. We have booked him through my company's speaker's bureau which you can learn about at www.TerrificSpeakers.com.

Allow us to introduce you to more exciting personalities who can and will bring you hope. Read this entire book!

Contact the other speakers you read about in this book for they all bring something unique and of great value to you and nearly any audience. Go-to www.TerrificSpeakers.com

You can give this book to your loved ones and friends—they will love you more as a result. (See the end of the book for an order form and order more copies—or contact the speaker direct from whom you got this book).

> **You can create a life with more hope…**
> **More success is yours as a result…**
> **I can guarantee it!**

(a sign for all to see)

God Saves And Restores Rodney!
BY: LISA BULDO

Something happened to me a few months ago that I want to share with you. Someone that I went to high school with got very sick and was in the hospital. His name is Rodney. I found out about it through an email. I sent a general reply, as did others, to say I'd pray for this man.

Later that evening the Word of Lord came to me saying He wanted *me* to go to the hospital the next day (which was over an hour drive), and to lay hands on this man and pray for him. I started to reason that I had not seen him in twenty-five years and I didn't know what I'd say, and maybe he would think I was crazy. But the Lord told me that He appointed me to go and do this. I was either going to *choose* to obey God, or not. I said "Yes, Lord, I'll go."

When I arrived at the hospital, Rodney was in CCU (Critical Care Unit), and his room was near the nurse's station. When I walked in, I immediately knew why the Lord sent me. Rodney was hooked up to all kinds of machines with a breathing apparatus down his throat. He had a bandage around his head, he was swollen from head to toe, and he was asleep, or so I thought. I tapped his left arm and called his name a few times to see if he'd wake up, and all of a sudden he took a deep breath but he didn't wake up. Just then one of the machines started going off loudly. After a minute or so, the loud noise stopped. He hadn't woken up, and no one came in the room. I got up and put one hand on his head, and the other on his chest, and I prayed in name of the Lord Jesus Christ of Nazareth for his healing. I declared that by the power and authority of Jesus' name, Rodney will LIVE and NOT die. I commanded sickness, disease and every evil thing that was trying to come against him and his body, to LEAVE in the name of Jesus, and to go back to hell where it belonged. I was bold in my prayer, and I felt a strong peace about it.

I found his mother in the nearby waiting room and introduced myself as a former classmate. I told her that I was sent there by the Spirit of God to pray for her son. I asked her what was wrong with Rodney. She said he had asthma, sleep apnea and he had gotten pneumonia. She said he had been unconscious for two weeks before I came. I told her that God had a specific message for her as well. I told her that God said that *she* has authority over her son's life, and NOT to let the devil steal her son's life. She was in tears as she told me they wanted to unplug him twice, but they didn't. Praise God. She said two days before I came, they were taking him to do a tracheotomy, but then they decided not to do it at the last minute because of his breathing. They weren't sure he would make it. God used me to bring *__Inspiring Hope!__*

She said she knew God sent me because the night before, she was praying and told God that she couldn't take it, and that *she* needed to be ministered to. God heard her cries and He knew that I would go, so He sent me.

I kept in touch with Rodney's mother over the next month or so, and then out of the blue one day, I called her and a man answered the phone, and she answered the phone at the same time. I said, "Hi, this is Lisa Buldo, and I'm calling to find out how Rodney is doing." The man said, "This is Rodney." I almost fell out of my chair! I was praising God, so ecstatic, as Rodney told me about how he's all better and doing great! Praise and thank GOD!

You need to know that as a child of Almighty God, YOU have authority over the Devil regarding yourself AND your family! Luke 10:19 says it clearly. When you take authority in Jesus' name, and be bold about it, you will be victorious! **Amen.**

Brian

By: Vitalia Bryn-Pundyk M.Ed. ACG/CL

How many of you recall an incident or an experience, a "turning point" if you will, that forever changed the way that you performed your job, raised your children, or even viewed others?

I remember my first year teaching Spanish at Brooklyn Junior High. I felt so unprepared because I didn't have any previous work experience except for supervised student-teaching. I was confident in my language abilities, excited to have my own classroom, and knew that I had great organizational skills, but I did not get enough classroom management training nor instruction in dealing with "special needs" students.

My classes were made up of very diverse students. They were all freshman close in age, but they represented different nationalities and learning abilities. I had black, white, Jewish, Asian and Hispanic students, as well as two or three that were labeled "LD" (learning disabled), and one student, a special needs student, with a physical disability. His challenge was muscular dystrophy.

As a Spanish teacher, it was really important for me to make language learning fun and a positive experience for all of my students. I always encouraged everyone to be actively involved with our classroom activities. I wanted my students to make daily progress in developing their language skills while enjoying the cultural aspect of each lesson.

Our cultural activities included a variety of fun experiences. For instance, "Friday Food Day!" We had students volunteer to bring in an assortment of wonderful ethnic dishes for our class to sample. We also had a regular schedule for viewing Spanish language films with English sub-titles. And once a month, we listened to music and practiced singing Mexican pop and folkloric songs, like "The Mexican Hat Dance," "La Bamba", and "La Cucaracha."

One day, I decided that instead of just singing along with the music, we would all get up and learn traditional Mexican dances, the kind that are performed by large groups at holiday festivities and at weddings. Oh, and let's not forget those popular line dances. Remember the "Macarena?" – Now, wouldn't that be fun!

In preparation for teaching this lesson, I did all of my research on costumes and traditional dances, located the necessary music, and even choreographed a few dances myself! I applied all of my "expert" organizational skills to developing a great lesson plan – yet the night before I was actually going to teach this lesson, I tossed and turned in bed because I was certain that I had forgotten something, or rather, as it turned out… someone! "Oh no!" I woke up in the middle of the night absolutely panicked. "What am I going to do with Brian? I forgot about Brian!"

I remember Brian and can picture him just as clearly as if I had talked to him yesterday. Brian was about 5 feet 5 inches tall, had sandy blond hair, warm, friendly brown eyes and the biggest crooked-toothed smile I saw every morning when I arrived to school.

Brian had a physical disability. He was my "special needs" student who suffered terribly from muscular dystrophy. His left leg was turned inward and twisted like a pretzel from the knee down. He limped and hobbled with an uneven rhythm down our hallways, yet always managed to get to class on time. He carried his heavy books over his shoulder in a leather backpack, or when he could manage it, balance them out in front, in between his chest and left arm. His right arm, useless – bent at the elbow, pressed against his side, with his fingers curved and wrist twisted upward, like a broken-winged bird, never to fly – yet that never kept him from reaching his educational goals. To me, Brian wasn't just a "special needs" student—he was remarkable! He truly was special.

I worried all night how I was going to handle the "dance" lesson. I had no training for "special needs" students. I didn't know how to make accommodations. Should I make him sit out and watch the others? Should I write him a pass to the library for that hour? Should I force him to dance and risk being laughed at by the others? Or maybe, (although it never happened), he would be absent that day. "Oh dear Lord," I prayed, "Please just this once, make him be absent."

Well sure enough, the next day I arrived at school only to find Brian was there to greet me with that big smile. "Buenos dias, Sra. Pundyk?" "Buenos dias, Brian." I replied, "Como estas?" After practicing several exchanges like this, I spoke privately with Brian about my plans for the day and offered what I thought was an excellent solution. I asked if he'd like to be my classroom "helper" and hit…. the "play" button on the tape recorder that day. "Yeah! Nice going there Vitalia," I thought sarcastically to myself. "Just give yourself a pat on the back for that one."

Brian looked at me and smiled compassionately, understanding that I seemed more uncomfortable over the dance situation than he. He said; "Mrs. Pundyk, if you don't mind, I think I'd like to try." "Try?" I asked in disbelief, "You mean… try?" as my mouth fell to the floor. "Yeah, I can try, can't I?" he asked. "Well sure, Brian." I responded. "That would be great!" He continued enthusiastically, "I can even get some of my buddies to help!"

That day, I realized that I was the student and Brian was the teacher. I learned a very valuable lesson – not to ever underestimate the abilities of someone with a physical challenge nor a learning disability, nor to ever discount how great their contributions can be. That day was a "turning point" in my career that forever changed how I viewed my students and how I taught the rest of my career.

Today, I recognize and honor the fact that each one of us has our own challenges. Let's remember, that no matter what the challenge, each one of us has our own incredible potential to achieve!

"The Road to Happiness - You're Gonna Make it After All"

By: Vitalia Bryn-Pundyk M.Ed. ACG/CL

Do you recall "The Mary Tyler Moore" show? "Who can turn the world on with her smile? Who can take a nothing day and make it all worthwhile? Well it's you girl and you should know it. With each and every little movement you show it. Love is all around, etc…" It was one of my favorites growing up.

The lyrics to "The Mary Tyler Moore" theme song are the lyrics I sing whenever I'm faced with having to get through an obstacle, a struggle, or have to overcome a challenge. Like anyone else, I've had my share of these, and singing the song helps to assure me that I will make it through somehow.

To give you an example of some of my own obstacles and struggles in life, sharing a little of my own background and personal history with you will give you a better perspective of my own views on happiness and life.

I grew up in what most people would regard as a "happy childhood." My parents were very affectionate, loving, and supportive. They provided me with the tools and education I needed in order to achieve my goals.

I came from a family of educators. My Great-Grandmother was a chemistry teacher, my Grandmother, a voice teacher, and my mother, an elementary teacher. Following in their footsteps, I became a high school Spanish teacher and college professor. The importance of education was a value instilled in me from the time I was very young. However, I can remember all the way back to elementary school struggling with my studies the first couple of years.

The biggest obstacle that was facing me at the time was that of the language barrier. You see, English is not my first language, nor is it my second. Today I speak five languages. English is my third. But with a lot of hard work and by applying my best effort to earn good grades, I managed to finish high school early, and at the tender age of sixteen, I graduated two years ahead of my class.

I graduated from the University of Minnesota with a Bachelor's degree in Spanish Education and a Masters degree in Second Languages and Cultures Education. Although it seems like I've been on the fast-track with regard to reaching my goals, nothing that I attained in life was without its own challenges, sacrifice, and struggles.

I've managed to secure high-paying administrative positions in the field of education, as well as lose them to consolidation and state-wide reorganization. I won several scholarship programs, beauty and talent pageants that made me eligible to compete at the 1990 Miss Minnesota/Miss America state level pageant. Although I didn't win, I was pleased to have placed as a top-ten semi finalist and was proud of the accomplishments that my hard work and effort had earned. Additionally, I've managed to start a business from the ground up, (an accelerated language school for business people and interested adults), and kept it operating for eight years, only to be faced with having to close it due to a personal crisis that forced a shut down of it all.

That brings me to one of my toughest challenges and what I would describe as one of the darkest periods of my life. The personal crisis I was referring to was that of my divorce. Throughout my life, overcoming obstacles and achieving goals was something to which I had always been accustomed - so you can imagine my shock, when my husband of nearly seven years woke up one Saturday morning, turned around to look at me and said; "I'm not happy. We fight too much. I need more time and space. I'm leaving this marriage."

Now, I knew we had our disagreements, but hey, that's normal. And yes, the arguing and fights caused some "ups and downs" in our marriage, but I thought that had to be normal too, right? After all, as long as we knew we loved each other, we were of course "happy."

When my husband said, **"I'm leaving this marriage – I'm not happy."** That was the first time I viewed myself as having failed at anything. I felt anger, sadness and terribly depressed over my failed marriage. For a while I thought that its demise had to have been my fault. I thought, at least according to what **he** said that it was **my** responsibility to make him happy, and apparently, I had failed. At this time I had the opposite of Inspired Hope!

Now although he was only 39 at the time - just between you and me, I think he was going through an early mid-life crisis. As for me, it became serious depression. I felt as if I had hit the lowest point in my life. For nearly three months, I never turned on any lights in my house, never opened a window, and couldn't even get to sleep without crying myself to it. I had a lot of financial obligations and responsibilities which was my only reason for ever stepping out of the house, and after work, I'd come right back home to a miserably cold and dark hole.

My temporary job as an adjunct Spanish Instructor was quickly coming to an end and I needed to look for another job to be able to support myself. However, I knew that no one would hire me if I were to continue in this depressed state. Then I recalled something that my mother once said. It had something to do with a lesson on setting goals and achievements. She always reminded me of the saying, "If it's going to be, it's up to me!"

I **decided** that I needed to be happy again. Happiness was all around me. I discovered that I could find happiness anytime right where I was. Location is irrelevant. No matter where I am, **it's up to me** to create my happy life. **I** am the author of my happy life story. I write the chapters and create my own destiny, my own happiness, and the outcomes of my life! And <u>nowhere</u> does it say that I'm responsible for the happiness of others!! We are all responsible for our own lives and we are each responsible for creating joy in it. The "Road to Happiness" begins with each one of us – the "Road to Happiness" is up to me.

While I was managing my business, I had no time for another job (except for the part time temporary adjunct Spanish teaching position) – so when my husband walked out, there was no additional income. That situation forced me to shut down my school to keep from financial ruin, and I began looking for full-time work so that I could support myself. My job search resulted in securing a full time teaching position requiring me to relocate the following semester from Minnesota to New Jersey.

On November 9, 1999, when our divorce became final, I informed my "ex" that he was finally going to get more "time and space" – (about 1100 miles more space!) – I was moving to New Jersey! The news hit him like a ton of bricks – oh, you just had to have been there. The shock and disbelief on his face was priceless, and it caused him to realize just how hasty he had been to walk out on the marriage.

Well after many tears and apologies, and I mean apologizing profusely to **both** my parents and me, he begged forgiveness and once again got down on his knee. Six weeks later we remarried "Vegas" style! I joke with him every now and then just to remind him, "Happy wife, Happy life." "No happy wife, no happy life."

I don't know where the road to happiness will lead, but I do know the road to happiness begins with me. During that entire dark period of my life (the summer of '99), I had one song that kept replaying in my mind. The last line of the song is "You're gonna make it after all…!"

Stop Signs

Vitalia Bryn-Pundyk M.Ed. ACG/CL

There are all kinds of signs that cause us to stop. Whenever we cross a busy intersection for example, we may encounter red, octagonal-shaped signs with white, block-lettering that simply spell out the word and legally command us to stop.

Sometimes driving through our local neighborhoods on a hot, summer day, we observe young business entrepreneurs set up a small folding table and a chair on their front lawns as they post up a crayon-decorated sign. (Now how many of us have never pulled over and stopped for a child's lemonade stand?) Or while driving through the same suburban neighborhoods, you notice the sign that reads, "this way to garage sale." If you're like I, your curiosity combined with your good bargaining and shopping sense, compels you to pull over and stop. Check things out. See what treasures you may find. After all, Minnesota has only two seasons....winter and garage sales!

And who among us doesn't know someone who has a son or daughter that participates in their high school marching band, or varsity dance line team? These students are usually trying to raise money for a trip somewhere and when we drive by one of these signs, "Car Wash", we feel obligated to stop and support their cause. We reason with ourselves that our car is filthy and needs a wash anyway, so we pull over and stop.

My point is there are all kinds of signs that cause us to stop, be it because we are required to do so by law, or because something entices us to do so through some sort of incentive. Perhaps, its just simple curiosity that causes us to stop. We all stop for traffic signs and chances are that at some time or another, we've all stopped for any of those other signs mentioned too. But I wonder, how many of us would stop if we saw someone holding up the torn cardboard sign that reads "homeless, please help."

I've encountered this sign many times throughout my travels from Atlantic City to LA, Salt Lake City to New Orleans, and even not far from where I lived as a young child in NE Minneapolis. Every time I encounter an individual holding up this sign, I want to stop. I see the holding up of this sign as that individual's cry for help. My husband just argues that it's a scam. I'll pull over and hand out a couple of dollars or whatever spare change I have. My husband will roll up the windows, lock the car doors, and just continue to look straight ahead. He thinks I'm a fool handing out the money. I tell him I'm able to sleep better at night when I do.

My husband and I live in a beautiful, luxurious townhouse in Lakeville, Minnesota. A study conducted in 2002 showed that residents of Lakeville have one of the highest average incomes in all of the state with its median income being $75,000.00. Lakeville is really a high, upper-end middle class community that is continuing to grow and build all kinds of new construction, (even in today's economy). So, you can imagine my surprise when recently on my way to a Toastmasters meeting, I saw a woman with long, fading blond, almost white hair, in her mid-50's, with her shoulders hunched over, wearing torn jeans, standing in the middle of Interstate 35 on the left-hand side, as you're heading north, just before the Crystal Lake Road exit. She was holding up the torn cardboard that read "Homeless, please help."

This woman really looked desperate. She appeared beat up, needed help, and you could just tell from her posture, the sad look on her face, her whole demeanor, that if someone didn't offer her help, she would not be able to hang on to even one more day.

I had been running late to the meeting and did not even see a place on the interstate where I could stop to offer any help. I really wanted to, but with the heavy rush hour traffic, and cars moving at a snail's pace, it was impossible to get into a closer lane. There was no shoulder on the left side where she was standing to be able to pull over, so I just remained in my car and continued on. For three days afterward, I thought about this poor woman and worried for her safety. I wondered if there had been anything I could do.

The following week, I was asked to prepare a speech for my Toastmasters meeting and that's when the answer came to me. Although I was unable to stop in the middle of the interstate to help out this individual, I could do something even more proactive. I could bring a greater awareness to others about this very topic, "homelessness".

Homelessness is a problem that affects many people in America. It can be caused by a variety of problems. The main cause is unaffordable housing for the poor. Some causes include mental illness, substance abuse, lack of incentives to work, poor work ethics, and/or lack of decent education, and a lack of *Inspiring Hope!*

The National Law Center for Homelessness and Poverty reports that over three million men, women, and children were homeless over the past year- about 300,000 chronically and the others temporarily. In many cases, people are in and out of the homeless system, which includes shelters, hospitals, the streets and prisons.

It is these chronic users of the system that utilize 90% of the resources devoted to the problem.

It has been reported that the type of assistance homeless adults felt they needed most were help finding a job, finding affordable housing, and help paying for a house. However, the main types of assistance they usually required were clothing, transportation, and help with public benefits. Few homeless actually receive help finding housing.

Today, when I see someone holding up a torn cardboard sign, I am reminded of the song, "Just Another Day in Paradise" by Phil Collins. "She calls out to the man in the street, Sir, can you help me? It's cold and I've nowhere to sleep, etc..." The lyrics continue, "He walks on, doesn't look back. He pretends he can't hear her. Starts to whistle as he crosses the street. Seems embarrassed to be there." In the song, Phil Collins reminds us to think twice because it's "Another day for you and me in Paradise."

Homelessness is largely an outcome of the shortage of affordable housing and an increase in the numbers of the poor. However, solutions to end homelessness already exist. We know we can help individual homeless people. We simply have to STOP, take notice, and decide we want to do it.

If anyone needs hope, it is the homeless! Who was it that originally said... "But if not for the grace of God, there go I!" God has a special love for the homeless, so must we.

(supports farming and active senior living)

The Lord's Footpoint Is Always In My Work, Whether I Realize It Or Not!

Carol Stevens

When I was young, I always wanted to be a teacher. I loved my teachers, and other than my parents, my teachers were probably the greatest role models I personally knew. From Sunday school to regular school, my teachers had a tremendous influence on me. My father told me I should get a job that would enable me to support myself, and we all knew teachers didn't get paid enough. So, I went to college and did the sensible thing, earning a business degree. I always figured I could go back for alternative certification if I wanted to do so later. Along the way, though, I found another career that truly suited me.

One thing I know is that everything in our lives happens for a reason. We don't always understand why when we're going through those tough times, but I believe the Lord has a plan that's much bigger and better than I can imagine. It's just not always too easy to let go of my own plans to discover what He has in store for me.

After college, I did the sensible thing once again and got a job in management for a large company. It was a wonderful training ground, and it gave me the chance to learn from mentors and teachers who were much different than my school teachers. I learned there were so many ways to learn. Just because I had a college degree did not mean I'd finished learning...in fact, I found the learning curve had accelerated. Now, I was learning how to put all those things I'd learned in school into real practice. I loved my boss, Frank, who truly approached his job like it was his duty to teach me everything he knew. I learned from Frank that with his sincere appreciation and recognition, I would work as hard as I could. When I made a mistake he would simply ask me what I learned from it, and then would reassure me that he had full confidence in my abilities. I learned so much from Frank. I also learned about how to manage by the "school of hard knocks," as I did my best to motivate my team of thirteen direct reports. I believe that's how I developed such a passion for leadership. Experiencing the daily trials of management on so many levels was exciting, motivating, and draining.

After several jobs in the company's management development program over six years, I was still struggling to find out what I wanted to do when I grew up! I loved managing people, but still possessed this intrinsic desire to be a teacher. I had conducted various training sessions over the years, and thought I would enjoy being a trainer. To do that, I had to seek a new career direction. That was scary, as I was rather invested in the management career I had begun. My husband and I were hoping to start a family, and had been fighting the disappointment that comes with that dream not happening quickly enough for us (working on *our* plan, of course!). After praying for direction, I found myself leaving the stable, predictable world of the large corporation to embark on a new career as a trainer for a small, growing company.

The funny thing was that as soon as I changed jobs, just when I'd given up the idea of trying to get pregnant for a while, I learned I was expecting a child. I proceeded to gain several certifications to build my training tool set, and expected to return to the corporate world soon after having the baby.

You would think that by that time I would have learned to trust the Lord, his plan, and his timing, but I was in for more surprises! While I was out of maternity leave enjoying my wonderful infant son, I learned the scope of my job had changed and that I would need to travel frequently for the job. I was not interested in leaving my son one more minute than necessary, and had burned out on traveling back when I was in corporate management. So, my boss at the time invented a temporary part-time position for me. As things progressed, I began to realize I could accomplish my work tasks at home by working as a contractor. And that is how, over a decade ago, I began my company.

Now as I look back I see so much in the Lord's plan that helped me follow this path. At the time it was hard not to feel aimless, and question what to do next. Through it all, the Lord has provided, and I have seen His providence in all my trials.

When I decided to become a trainer, I worried about putting myself out there in front of constant audiences, and then asking them to evaluate me. I loved it so much, though, that I was willing to get over my insecurities. To this day, I still pray before each session, that the words will flow, the message will be clear, and that the lives of my class participants will be positively impacted as a result of spending time with me. Doing so has been incredibly affirming, and I have felt the Lord's presence with me as I struggled to give my best possible effort.

There are a few things I have learned about life from teaching others:

First, it truly is our thoughts today that will determine our future path, and how we approach our future makes all the difference! Today is a gift, and yet we often spend so much time worrying about either the past or potential future events that we fail to embrace it. So many participants in my sessions relate to this, and it's so interesting to hear their comments and insights when they really think about how they are using their energy.

Second, being a great leader is not a result of superior intelligence, scholastic aptitude, or formal education and experience. It's all about your attitude! Over the years I have had countless executives and middle managers who have tremendous academic pedigrees, and yet have never learned the people skills necessary to engage their employees. Traditional management was authority-driven, and many executives who grew up in that culture have struggled to "evolve" and develop the emotional competencies to truly know their employees. And we wonder why there is such a chasm between managers and employees in this nation. Here's the great news! Everyone has just what's needed to not only survive, but *thrive*, in today's environment. A little dose of self-awareness goes a long way toward becoming more effective with people. I once worked with an executive who was amazed when we discussed the blind spots that we have when it comes to our relations with others. He said he had never thought about his drive and ambition in quite that way, and said just looking at his behaviors and motivations in a different way transformed his relationships with his wife and his employees. It was incredible to see how this self-awareness helped him! He said he had been in management for over 20 years, and that he was living proof that you are never too old or set in your ways to change! Stories like that give me hope that it's never too late to change and that even though we might not see the immediate impact of what we are doing, you never know when your words might help someone in profound ways. Who are you influencing? Might you be influencing someone and not even be aware of it?

Third, trainers often have a lot of ego wrapped up in their success. However, I have found that I truly do my best work when I give it up to God. When I pray for my words to flow and touch someone's heart that is when the Lord blesses me with amazing connection opportunities. Staying close to the Lord keeps me humble, and reminds me that my blessings in my work are directly from Him, and no one else. When my participants' needs and feelings are considered to be as important as or more important than mine that is when great things happen. I once had a participant in a session tell me that I was the first person that helped her understand herself in such a way that she could feel okay being herself. She was very shy, and tended to focus on details and was known as somewhat of a perfectionist. All her life people had told her she needed to be more outgoing and sociable. I'm not sure when it became so popular to try to make people into someone they aren't, but that's a really tough way to live. What if we all sought to understand each other's strengths and nurture those more, while criticizing our flaws less. If I approached my vocation in a self-centered way, trying to "fix people" with my "expertise," that might make me feel important, but it wouldn't help their self-esteem at all. What if we all could raise the self-worth of those around us a little bit? What if we could love ourselves a little more and raise our own self-concept? What a wonderful world we would live in if that were the case.

Finally, if you pray for the Lord to direct and lead you along life's path, you will get there with much less angst! We don't always know why we are dealt the challenges that our lives bring us. In the midst of the storm it is difficult to know how we will be blessed or why we must endure these challenges. When we emerge from the trial on the other side, though, we can usually see a direct benefit we received from the trial...*if* we look for it. I believe that is the power of hope, why we continue to have it, and why it's so vital to our existence! There have been times when I didn't have enough business, and while I get frustrated in those moments, I can look back and see exactly why things were the way they were. More often than not, when I have had a free schedule, something has happened in my personal life that has required my attention. My children or spouse might have been ill, a family member or friend needed me, or I needed to recharge my batteries and refocus. If we are miserable in those moments, just waiting for things to change and get back to "normal," we may miss the lessons and blessings the Lord has in store for us in these times. And most importantly, the Lord has *always* provided for my needs in these situations thanks in large part to His ***Inspiring Hope!***

When we don't know how we will save enough money for our children to have presents under the Christmas tree or how we will pay the bills, a blessing always comes. It's not necessarily the same blessing we might have expected, and it doesn't always occur in our preferred timeframe, but it *does* come – if we are ready to receive it. I believe we'll be about as happy and fulfilled as we make up our minds to be. It's easy to spend some much time worrying that we fail to see the blessings in the present. Trusting in a higher power is a really tough thing to do, especially for someone like me who enjoys being in control. When I look back on my life so far, though, I definitely see that when I gave my circumstances up to God, though, things worked out much better than I could have imagined. I am still struggling with letting go, but it is getting easier as I learn to trust that no matter what comes my way I will be able to handle it if I keep my focus on the right things.

My life is an adventure to be continued…I don't know where the Lord will lead me next, but I am excited about the possibilities while living in *Inspired Hope!*

Change the "m" in home to "p" and you have
a better home because you have hope.

True Hope

By Lorna Millan Lisk, MS

At about 10 o'clock one evening, my first husband Ness (Nestor, his real name) was bending over with extreme pain in his chest. I called the ambulance and in 15 minutes we were in the intensive care unit of Good Samaritan Hospital in Zanesville, Ohio. This was one of two hospitals where Ness sent his patients as a practicing pediatrician in that town. All along I was in constant prayer.

As I sat in the waiting room beside the ICU in extreme sorrow and with tears rolling down my cheeks, a priest came and spoke to me words of comfort. He narrated how he survived his heart attack ten years earlier. To me, he was sent by God and this gave me hope. I fell asleep where I was seated. Thank God, our sons who were ages 10, 14 and 15 were able to take care of themselves. If needed, they could call on their friends' parents who were our next-door neighbors.

When I woke up, it was almost dawn. I checked on Ness who was connected to a respirator and it was apparent that his condition remained the same. I walked to the chapel and I was quietly crying while in deep prayer. A nun walked over to me and gave me tissues to wipe my tears. After thanking her, I uttered words of gratitude to God again for this other sign of hope from Him. These hopeful manifestations implanted me with vigor and peace at an almost unbearable time such as this.

I hurried back to ICU where Ness was, but lo and behold, right before me was a most dreadful sight! A number of doctors and nurses swarmed around him. They were coding him or applying electric shock through his body to save his life. I could not bear the sight, so I rushed to the next room and cried loudly. Continuous flow of tears cascaded into a huge pool in front of me.

Eleven hours after we entered the hospital, a doctor came into the room where I was but swiftly exited probably frightened by my loud sobbing. Right after him came another doctor who was our friend. He broke the most painful and tragic news in my life. Our Lord took away Ness forever. **I felt like the whole world crushed on me and I wailed louder than ever uncontrollably. The pain was horrendous.**

The next morning I could no longer cry, but this time I was devoid of hope. I told our Lord mentally that I wanted to die also. Startling me was His instant reply by His Holy Spirit, "You should be thankful for the many happy married years I gave you."

I smiled and mentally responded, "That's right, Lord. A world of thanks to You. I thank You also for Ness was a wonderful man, husband and doctor and so are my three sons. I thank you for life, good health and for being a marvelous Provider for our needs and handing me opportunities to serve You."

The foregoing miraculously and instantly transformed my despair into inner peace and baffling joy. God infused me with incredible strength to go on with my life with my three sons. By His grace, all of them have become successful practicing physicians. Eight years after our Lord took Ness, He bestowed me another wonderful husband, Thomas, successful owner of Professional Speakers Bureau International (see www.terrificspeakers.com) and author. God inspired me to serve Him and others in various ways including my international healing ministry after working as a chemical engineer and chemist early in my adult life. I have been a speaker in several countries and numerous states in U.S., founder of Worldwide United Prayer for Christ and Catholic Woman of the Year in 2002 for the 23-county Columbus, Ohio diocese.

Indeed, I found that even in our darkest and hopeless moments, God will rush to our aid if we pray, love, thank and serve Him and His children. Jesus is my awesome Savior, Provider and my true Hope!

(happy family life)

Adding Health Equals Greater Wealth

Angela Gracia Smith

The wealth of life begins with abundant health. A very simple and profound truth that I discovered is my health is my greatest wealth. To acquire this, I must invest in my health wisely through habits that I call "deposits." This is also true for you. You can enjoy a greater return on life when you are rich with health and wellness.

In my experience, true wealth is when my spiritual, mental and physical wellbeing are functioning well. This God-given gift is worth protecting and promoting. It is something to value greatly and not to be ignored. We must deposit life-adding habits every day that will promote a vibrant and thriving life during each season.

As our news headlines highlight, material wealth can disappear quickly. Markets change rapidly and people can lose what once appeared to be secure and prosperous long-term financial investments. Likewise, our health can also be lost through poor investments and decision-making. Thankfully, with commitment and self-discipline, our health can be maintained for the long run.

I have developed an investment plan and strategy based on the principle that adding health is gaining wealth. One of my slogans is "adding health to life." My personal health investment plan answers this question: "What can I do regularly to add health to my life?" My answers include using my faith in Jesus Christ, spending time with my husband, purchasing and preparing for boosting wellness, taking time for exercise, and consuming certain dietary supplements on a regular basis.

My investment strategies are simple techniques or habits that help me attain my personal health investment plan. For example, when I travel I carry supplements in my handbag for easy access. I purchase and use comfortable shoes so that I can easily walk at any time or any place. I keep a portable music device in my purse loaded with praise and worship music that enriches my life as I listen to it. These and other simple strategies help me to remain faithful to the habits that add health to my life.

During a recent seminar, a participant said that he did not want to live to be "old" and be a burden for his family. "Not a wise way to look at living a long life," I thought. Instead of focusing on his options and opportunities for achieving excellent health and maintaining his body in good working condition, he was dreading his "old" age as a hassle to be avoided. That was not *Inspiring Hope!*

Thankfully there are men and women like Mr. and Mrs. Jack Lalanne! They are fantastic role models for living in optimal physical and mental condition at an advanced age. Jack Lalanne pioneered televised fitness programming and he is well into his 90's. He and his wife are still promoting the message of living life at its fullest. This couple is making the art of aging a successful reality for all of us who desire to live long healthy years. We can learn from people like these.

Two deposits the Lalanne couple makes each day as a part of their health investment plan include eating living foods and exercising. One of their strategies is being promoted regularly on television infomercials. In order to consume living foods like fresh vegetables and fruits, this couple practices juicing. To be able to exercise, this couple has a gym in their home that they use daily.

If you want to live each day to enjoy the fruit of your labor, you must decide that your state of wellbeing is a priority. It has been said that early in life people give up their health to gain wealth and later in life, they give up their wealth to regain their health. The truth is that gaining and maintaining health can be a simple and inexpensive process.

Each positive step taken at any age will produce benefits that your body will thank you for. For example, eating more fresh vegetables enriches your body with the nutrients it needs to repair damage and increase performance. As a result, when you eat more fresh vegetables, you have more energy and vigor. Like Jack Lalanne, I also include homemade vegetable juices in my regular food choices. One of my favorite green juices has cucumbers, celery, cilantro or parsley, kale, spinach or dandelion, lemon or lime, a little ginger and a bit of garlic… I know it is not your common juice, but it sure is delicious and my body just loves it as I have already reaped several benefits from this habit.

Other good habits that I deposit regularly are drinking warm filtered water with fresh squeezed lemon or lime upon awakening in the morning. I add raw apple cider vinegar to my drinking water. I learned these ideas from reading books like *Become Younger* by Norman Walker and *Bragg Healthy Lifestyle* by Paul and Patricia Bragg. I also do a few stretches so that my muscles can remain limber. These health deposits don't take very long and are very economical. The overall improvements I have derived are worth every minute I take to do each activity! From better digestion to more flexibility and mobility, the benefits are real and valuable.

New horizons can open up for you when you make your health a priority! You may visit the world with your taste buds as you explore Chinese, Italian, Greek, American, Cuban and other types of interesting cuisine that offer nutritious options. You can get active in walking, cycling or running clubs and meet people that are new and exciting. In short, making health your greatest wealth is an adventure that enriches your life in ways you can only enjoy!

Remember - **Adding health equals greater wealth!** Simple, economical and wise investments will yield returns that make living more rewarding. Be wise and choose life-adding habits more regularly than those habits that subtract health. Improve your wealth of health by developing your personal action plan. Consider multiple strategies for remaining consistent and faithful to your health goals. Your body will say thank you now and throughout each new season that arrives. I hope you have a healthy long life!

Forward in Hope!
The Beatitudes Create Stories of Hope for More Success
Dr. Thom A. Lisk

"Let's look forward in hope that the best is yet to be." Minister Michael Watson asserted this sentence during his December 31, 2008 send-off into the future. Everyone needs hope, he was not simply mouthing what people wanted to hear or needed to hear, he was prayerfully stating a fact that seems to be planted in every human heart: that is that a bright and wonderful future is something worth hoping for.

Yet sometimes as we look around at our present circumstances we can be discouraged or disappointed, and we find we must be careful that these attitudes in the present moments of our lives, do not negatively affect our futures. This is very important to remember.

One of the great reasons to generate in our lives a very positive hope, yes in-spite of circumstances that can scream otherwise, is that we affect the future by our attitudes in the now. Attitudes are often more than simple, yet important, thoughts. Attitudes in the now can change the future for the better, or for the worse. **You decide!**

Looking forward hopefully at the beginning of a new year is a common normal thing to do. **How about today?!**—today is the first day in the rest of your life!—today is the most important day in your life!

Establishing from your positive hopes actionable goals to change yourself and your environments for the better, doing so permanently, is not common—it is uncommon and hard work. You can be (if not already) an uncommon winner.

Recognizable examples include the New Years Resolution to loose weight; have you done that before? Or how about beginning a new exercise program at the beginning of a new week? For many years I ran in a local 5K (3.1 miles) race which started at 11:30 p.m. on 12/31 so I, and dozens of other brave souls, would finish the year positioned for success.

> Positioning yourself for more success always begins with hopeful attitudes and then takes the form of better action. Sustaining a positive energized effort is often the biggest challenge. What runs through your head when someone mentions the word attitude? What are the best attitudes?

The Beatitudes

Are you familiar for your own personal application with the famous nine beatitudes given by Jesus as recorded in Matthew chapter 5 beginning with verse 3? Please read as follows in a prayerful meditative state. Then consider my comments I intended for your betterment.

1. Blessed are the poor in spirit, for theirs is the kingdom of heaven.

2. Blessed are they who mourn, for they will be comforted.

3. Blessed are the meek, for they will inherit the land.

4. Blessed are they who hunger and thirst for righteousness, for they will be satisfied.

5. Blessed are the merciful for they will be shown mercy.

6. Blessed are the clean of heart, for they will see God.

7. Blessed are the peacemakers, for they will be called children of God.

8. Blessed are they who are persecuted for the sake of righteousness, for theirs is the kingdom of heaven.

9. Blessed are you when they insult you and persecute you and utter every kind of evil against you (falsely) because of Me. Rejoice and be glad, for your reward will be great in heaven. Thus they persecuted the prophets who were before you.

(Matthew 5: 3-12, The New American Bible, St. Joseph Edition)

More sermons on these nine verses through the past nearly 2000 years have been given I suppose than possibly on any other portion of Holy Scripture. I ask myself what do I have to add to what already has been shared? And, do I dare attempt to interpret the Word of God word for word?

Words are powerful things and the most important and powerful words are found in the Holy Bible. Words shape our thoughts, which in turn shape our actions. Actions then in turn create habits, and habits next create what can be called our character. Lastly…Character determines destiny.

I mentioned to begin this chapter it was the beginning of a new year when I began writing. It is now January 28th. I have done many things for this book project however in nearly four weeks I did nothing to this chapter other than write the first page up to the sub heading: Beatitudes.

Why do all of us not do more everyday towards our goals?

Some days we have more hopelessness than hopefulness if the truth were known. It is not simply the excuse of, "other priorities", in many instances. I have written other books, and as I can thankfully recall, I wanted to give-up several times during the process of the writing. My attitudes were not always as they needed to be. Know the experience? What can we do to keep the right attitude all the time?

> **One prescription that works is to memorize and apply daily the nine beatitudes. To help you towards this goal, what follows is nine stories with a few carefully chosen words for your personal edification about each beatitude.**

Blessed are the poor in spirit...

Who in our world today really wants to be "poor in spirit"? What was Jesus—the God-man and second person of the Trinity—driving at with this directive? I've surveyed people and read various expert teachings and conclude as follows. God loves us so much that HE wants us to respond with love and devotion for HIM, not just once in awhile but at all times we are to honor and love God. "Poor in spirit" appears to be someone who truly relies on God, not in self.

Story of Hope: By the grace of God, over the years I have been so blessed to meet many outstanding and successful people, some of whom you'd consider famous. Upon reflection, I realize now that the people we often admire the most are the people who are the most dependent on God. Think about it! Seldom do people come right out and say, "I am dependent on God!" However the greatest among us are those who are the most humbly living for God, not themselves, as evidence by the sacrifices they make to achieve their "greatness." Your story about a hero might be worth sharing. My greatest story is the story of Jesus: God's #1 example of sacrificial love. Jesus became "poor in spirit" so you and I could have our spirits united with God, now and forever. We are poor in spirit when we likewise sacrifice for those we love and serve.

Blessed are they who mourn

This important attitude placed into action seems more doable than some of the other nine. It is easy to mourn over the loss of a loved one, as an example, however we have much more to mourn than the loss of those we have loved and/or known. In recent months people have been mourning the loss of their hoped for and worked for financial security. The best solution?—help and comfort other people: give others ideas on how to recover.

Story of Hope: Your story about a loss of a loved one in your life may be very meaningful to you. At Church Sunday after Mass where I served as Lector along with my wife Lorna, I encountered Jack in the lobby or as we call it, Marian Hall. We did some good nature kidding of each other, mostly having to do with age, so I asked Jack, "How old are you?"

When he told me 80 out of his one good eye, (he is blind in the other) I told him, "Jack, I hope you live another 20 years!" To which Jack laughed as if he would be glad to have another day, week or month. I then told him the story of my maternal grandmother who lived to age 105—this was an effort on my part to give him hope. I told Jack, "I sure did mourn when she died, however, I will never forget shortly before she graduated to the next life, Grandma telling me, 'Thom, look at me, I am worn out, I think God has forgotten me! What use am I to anyone anyway?"

"Forgotten you, Grandma!? Please don't think or say that! We need you. You are a great example to all of us, and besides, you can pray for me! Please pray for me!" I implored her. In some ways I was already mourning the inevitable that took place not many months later, and I was prayerfully working to apply the b-attitude not to my loved ones who would all mourn grandma's passing, but offer some comforting words now while I still could.

You can find people in all walks of life that you can comfort, people who need your help. God promises to bless you now as you offer comfort and hope to others. And additionally, when you later need comfort or more hope in your life, you are paying forward so that you will get the comfort—the hope—you need during your darkest days.

Blessed are the meek

What did the Lord mean by "meek"? I have known positive examples of meek people in my life and I realize their personalities are attractive, actually appealing. A good word to describe a meek person is transparent. Meek is not weak. Meek can be very strong. Meek is not self-centere. Meek is God and other people contented.

Story of Hope: A meek person can be a very successful person, a person who "inherits the land." In the days of Jesus, land was a precious commodity. The people he was talking to were an occupied people. Roman soldiers were a constant reminder of their lack of control over their own destiny, or so it seemed. They most likely were not helpful about "inheriting any land." Jesus preached non-violence, to "turn the other cheek." He knew they could not win through violence or force. A meek person is not looking for a fight.

I have a business acquaintance who is a successful man who admits to being "very aggressive." He's smart and hardworking, that is primarily why he has accumulated so much wealth. He looks only for "distressed assets" to acquire and pursues them aggressively. He is meek alright. Maybe just like the people who got wealthy during the great depression of the 1930's or when people who lost their land through foreclosure, some people bought land and held it at 10-25% of the earlier value. Meek people patiently wait on God's opportunities and seem to capitalize best. Can you do the same?

Blessed are they who hunger and thirst for righteousness

It is important to realize that all of these beatitudes have associated with them a promise. You could call it a conditional promise but none-the-less God is promising us something of significance with each of the nine beatitudes.

Story of Hope: I was provided a free night's lodging at a five diamond hotel, The Island Hotel, Newport Beach to do a site inspection to bring a group event to this location. At about 7pm my hunger was not for food but for God. So I asked about the nearest Catholic Church and set out to jog the 1.1 miles. When I arrived I found an empty church inviting me to pray, meditation, and scripture reading. At the end of my time in the church, I found right thinking about several important current issues in my life. I jogged back to my hotel; my most important hunger abated, and decided to skip dinner and rather to fast from food so I could better enjoy the beauty of what surrounded me.

The human person has many drives and many diverse motivations, however, none are more important than the pursuit of righteousness or right thinking. Right thinking is hopeful thinking, an approach that says, "Yes, there is always the right and best solution to every problem." Don't settle for second best unless that is perfectly right for you right now. Keep up-grading your standards, this is also right.

Blessed are the merciful

It is not always easy to show mercy, have you noticed? My human tendency is to want to get even with people who have hurt me. Rather I am to try to understand why they might have hurt me and show them mercy. How hard is that? Seems like I must always be asking why questions to get to the bottom of what is going on around me; or, through me or by me for that matter, too.

Story of Hope: Offering mercy can be a simple comfort for people. It is more than mourning with someone. Mercy is a great gift from God. When you show mercy to people, you are helping people to experience one of the best characteristics of our loving God, and in offering mercy, you may be most like God.

You forgive and you will be forgiven. Who is the person or persons who have hurt you the most in your life? Offer those people mercy and total forgiveness and you will find healing and more forgiveness in your own life. It may be hard for you to talk about those who have hurt you the most. Journaling or writing your thoughts may start out as an expression of anger; however, pray that as you vent your emotions, you are able to find mercy to show to the persons that you may even consider your enemy.

Divorce is for many one of the most difficult experiences in their entire lifetimes. I spoke to Tim on the phone one recent Saturday, and he told me about the demands of his wife, and how he could not send me the money he owed me or our company due to the predicament he was experiencing. I wanted to show Tim mercy, help him to forgive her, so he could experience God's love and healing, but he already seemed to have it all figured out. In so many words, he told me that "Women are always right." The fact that this was his third marriage reminded me that people are doomed to repeat the same mistakes over and over again if they do not find the correct ways to deal with their problems.

The correct way is always God's way, and God's way is total forgiveness, offering mercy and not holding grudges. We must get better, never bitter. We must admit our mistakes and behaviors that cause people to sometimes treat us as they do. If we want better outcomes, we must look at ourselves and think "How can I change?" Offering mercy to ourselves is often necessary to permanent improvement. Tim needs to be much less of the macho man, and be willing to say, "Please forgive me?" Helping other people to love us unconditionally starts when we love ourselves first.

Blessed are the clean in heart

Now this is one of the nine beatitudes that makes a lot of sense to me maybe because I have experienced the opposite—an unclean heart. Thankfully I know how to pray and work to keep my heart clear and clean and the benefits of doing so.

Story of Hope: Ash Wednesday 2009 I awoke to unusual dreams and visions which had been going on for I estimated about an hour before I decided I'd be wise to get up and prayerfully attempt to discern what was going on in my life. At 3am I began to write. I was in a 5 diamond resort hotel at the time provided to me free for a night to consider bringing a group event to the Langdon Huntington in Pasadena. One thing I wrote to the Bishop in Columbus, Ohio was rather prophetic in some ways as I noted that my visions of me being nailed to a cross (like Jesus had been) brought about tears, deep sorrow, and repentance. After writing the three page letter was complete (try this!) I experienced a very clean heart. My thoughts seemed so purified that I didn't miss the sleep; I was very ready for 6:30am mass at St. Phillip the Apostle Church.

Repentance is always a key to creating a clean heart so we are positioned to serve more and better. After mass, back in my hotel room before an 8am meeting, clarity of thought flowed onto paper so that this writing seems extremely important for future readers. You too can see things clearer and make better decisions from a cleaner heart.

Blessed are the peacemakers

If you are the parent of two or more children as I am, you know the role of peacemaker up-close and personal. We read about or hear on TV about efforts in peacemaking. How can we be peacemakers in our own lives day in and day out?

Story of Hope: You will benefit from reading the writings of Chic Dambach who appears elsewhere in this book. Chic was the Director of the famous International Peace Corps. His story is one of hope realized as a boy who graduated from Thomas Worthington High School with idealistic ideals to make a difference. And, he did, and still does. At his 40th high school graduation reunion, or near to it, he received an alumni award that shows how peacemakers are vitally important—blessed—and rewarded in practical ways.

The teacher who intervenes when certain students are quarrelling is a peacemaker. The parent who separates siblings who are arguing over "mine" is making peace. The boss who builds teamwork in his office or work place brings harmony to people and the workplace, and increased productivity and maybe profitably is a result. You can be a peace maker in a variety of simple roles in your life and make this a better place as a result. Do so habitually and there is no telling how many rewards you will receive.

Blessed are they who are persecuted

From time to time I suppose we all can feel a little bit persecuted in our lives. In other words we are wrongly judged or evaluated, or so we think. Rather than judge in return or act inappropriately have you learned this important lesson? Think right and act right towards those who judge you and you will find great peace, maybe even a bit of heaven on earth!

Story of Hope: None of us like to be persecuted although some people bring persecution, rightfully so, upon themselves as they stand strong for what is right. At other times and in some places, people think they are standing strong for the right cause, as an example, and they are persecuted and they lose everything as a result.

Through my company, Professional Speakers Bureau Int'l, we got a request for Dr. Bernard Nathanson to speak to a pro-life college group in North Carolina. Now here is a man that has been persecuted both for being wrong, and then later for being right. Briefly, his story is that he was an abortionist who performed thousands of abortions. After many years of some activity, he saw an ultrasound picture of a baby in the womb of a mother, and finally came to the right position, "Yes, that is a baby!"

He had been persecuted up to that point by pro-life activists, and now after his repentance for his "murder of thousands of innocent lives", he became a pro-life Catholic. For several years until failing health caught up with him, he spoke to groups about evils of abortion, and he was persecuted for doing so by the pro-choice side of the issue. Only when his persecution for righteousness sake was in alignment with the b-attitude that Jesus taught in His Sermon on the Mount, was he doing God' will and setting himself up for the most important rewards: not the financial rewards from his dastardly earlier deeds, but rather eternal rewards in heaven and peace from a clear conscience at the time of death.

Let's get ourselves as right as possible before it is too late. When we are "right" we can generate the best kind of hope, a hope in God and His (the best!) reward system.

Blessed are they when they insult you...

As a professional speaker for 32 years, as well as someone who speaks for free in the church and for community groups, and as someone who has marketed and booked other pro speakers wanting to earn income for their life-improving and/or important messages, it never ceases to amaze me how in the same audience you have someone who loves you and rates you a 10 (highest) and someone else in the same audience who rates you a 1 (lowest). That's part of the game. Although we'd all like to be rated a few by everyone all the time, you haven't tried hard enough, most likely, if you haven't been ridiculed, insulted, or worse.

Story of Hope: If you play it safe all the time, never willing to take risks, you may not generate many insults in your life. On the other hand, take risks and you may fail, and your failures may be accompanied by insults. Like in the story of the life of Jesus, you might be perfectly right; however your message may be misunderstood. And your challenge to change may bring upon you insult. Be happy!

I hesitate to reflect on the times I've been insulted in my life and share those insults specifically. Some are too painful to review. I can share for your benefit, that in each case, as I turned to God or His Word, and/or the church, in prayer, my wisdom and understanding broadened and deepened, and I became better able to help other people.

If I was rightly insulted and deserved the insult or criticisms, I need to be happy, take it to heart as corrective, and then change myself, with the help of God, for the better.

If, as in this last b-attitude as taught by Jesus, I am insulted for adhering to a strong faith in Jesus and what He teaches, living my life for Him first and foremost, then the insults are very much worth it. See God in heaven saying to you – this is what I see – upon arrival…

"Well done good and faithful servant… enter in your eternal reward." Paradise! Hope fulfilled!

(supportive of handicapped citizens)

The Power of A Loving Touch

By Dr. Charles D. Schmitz and Dr. Elizabeth A. Schmitz

*Touching becomes kind of a **Morse Code**—a substitute for language and the expression of feeling. Successfully married couples have mastered the **Morse Code** of marriage – it's called "loving touching".*

We have been married for 42 years and simply can't keep our hands off of each other! For many years, we thought we were unique. Then we started our research for our book, and did we get a big surprise -- virtually every happily married coupled we interviewed reported the same condition! Over time we have come to call it the "tactile response." Literally translated, it means, "I touch you here, I touch you there, I touch you everywhere!"

During our interviews with married couples we pay a lot of attention to their tactile interactions. More often than not, they sit on the couch during the interview and hold hands or place some part of their body on their mate's body. It is their way of saying "I love you so much I simply must touch you." So why all of this touching? As part of our interviews we asked the couples to tell us what they believe to be the most endearing and important characteristics of their spouse. We continued with the following questions: "How would you describe your spouse? What adjectives would you use?" Here are the words we most often heard: encouraging, positive, loving, honest, has integrity, beautiful (or handsome), understanding, wonderful, patient, loves life, loves me, unselfish, giving, caring, trusting, generous, helpful, conscientious, and humorous. Words to live by in a marriage wouldn't you say? And they said these things unabashedly, without apologies.

> Successful couples know nearly everything about each other. They have studied in infinite detail how their spouse looks, feels and acts. They know what makes the one they love tick and can recite in scripture and verse their best qualities. They brag about each other all the time. They love each other for a whole bunch of reasons and don't mind telling you what they are. Successful couples stay focused on the positive, what's to love!

What do their words about each other have to do with touching? Here's what we observed during our many interviews—when couples told us something special about their spouse in response to our questions, they would touch each other as if to emphasize the impotance of the words. Touching was like an exclamation mark! Over time, we believe that these couples, like the two of us, say these words with a touch without always saying the words out loud. Touching becomes kind of a *Morse Code*—a substitute for language and the expression of feeling. Successfully married couples have mastered the *Morse Code* of marriage – it's called touching.

A wise person once said that if you pass your spouse 100 times a day, you should touch them 100 times a day. When you touch someone, you are acknowledging his or her presence and expressing your love. In effect you are saying, "I love you so much I simply must touch you." That powerful message of love is sent every time a simple touch happens.

The hundreds of successfully married couples we have interviewed over the past 25 years understood early in their marriages about the power of touching. Towanda and Shawn are convinced that they would never have made it to their 31st anniversary if they had not understood the power of a simple touch, when a drunk driver almost ended their loving journey together.

As they were returning home from a marvelous evening at a local fund-raiser, a drunk driver hit their Toyota head-on at well over 50 miles per hour. Luckily neither of them has any memory of the accident after seeing the car coming straight toward them. They were spared the pain and horror of the hours immediately following the crash.

Towanda and Shawn were transported by helicopter to the trauma center at Baptist Hospital. Within about three days, Shawn was able to sit up in the hospital bed, but it would be several months before he would regain his strength and have full movement of his legs and his left arm. However, Towanda was not as fortunate. She had sustained major head trauma and had internal bleeding, leaving Towanda in a coma. The doctors were not optimistic about her recovery, indicating that Towanda had been in a coma for three days with no signs of improvement.

The impact of the doctor's prognosis for Towanda was beginning to sink into Shawn's consciousness even though he was battling his own physical and psychological problems from the accident. How would he ever survive without his love of 27 years? It just wasn't possible to think about. Shawn felt like he had been knocked off balance and unable to process mentally what was happening. Their perfect life was in ashes as they both lay in their separate hospital beds, two floors apart due to the nature of their injuries. How could this be happening to them? They loved each other so much, yet in one instant a drunk driver could destroy everything. Shawn tried to figure out what he should do?

It took about a week before Shawn was able to get into a wheel chair long enough to visit Towanda in her hospital room. There she lay—still and silent—not even breathing on her own. She had so many bruises on her face that Shawn hardly recognized her. The first thing Shawn did was to get close enough to Towanda's bed to get hold of her hand and just hold it tight in his own hand. He spent the next hour just sitting there talking to Towanda while continuing to hold her hand. Shawn was looking for any signs of movement or recognition in her face, eyes, hands, or anywhere. Nothing!

Each day while Shawn was working hard to recover himself, he would find a way to wheel himself down to Towanda's room to hold her hand. After a week, he gained enough flexibility to be able to lean over to kiss her on the cheek. Each visit was longer in duration and allowed him the opportunity to touch Towanda's hands, arms and cheeks as he kept telling her how much he loved her and what they were going to do when they left the hospital together. Day after day as Shawn slowly regained his own strength, he saw no signs of change in Towanda. Yet, he spent longer and longer amounts of time just holding her hands and touching her face, as he talked to her about their wonderful lives together.

One day as he was rubbing her arms, one of her doctors came in and sat down to visit with him. Shawn's fear was that he wanted to discuss the eventual removal of the life support systems. Instead, the doctor spoke very softly about the power of touch. It seems that he had spent valuable time with eminent doctors from other countries who had witnessed first-hand the miracles of recovery when the patient was given no hope of survival. The doctors were convinced that some of their patients with a medical prognosis of no hope had been reached through the power of touch from a loved one. The doctor told Shawn that love and touch can have great healing powers at times when medicine provides no more answers, so he should not give up yet.

Little did the doctor know just how critical his timing had been for Shawn. It was just the encouragement he needed. Instead of taking the prognosis as a sentence of impending doom, Shawn set out to produce one of those miracles the doctor had talked about. He continued touching Towanda as often as he could get up and out of his own hospital bed. Day after day as he grew stronger, he wanted to share his strength with Towanda. Shawn just knew the doctor was right. Towanda could feel the power of his loving touch and it had to give her the strength to come back to him. It just had to work!

After 15 days, Shawn was ready to be released from the hospital. He needed 6 to 8 weeks of heavy-duty physical therapy before he could return to work even on a very limited basis. However, he knew that his release meant it would be more difficult to spend the needed time with Towanda since they lived almost one hour away from the hospital and he would not be allowed to drive for at least another month.

When the physical therapist and counselor came into his hospital room to talk to him about the plans after his release, he broke down from the overwhelming hopelessness of what he thought would be an impossible situation. Shawn credits these two caring individuals with turning Towanda and his entire situation around. After several phone calls, they arranged for Shawn to stay at a residence home for family members who needed to be close to their loved ones and had no means of transportation. With that placement came a full support system of other caring individuals for everything he would need. At that moment, Shawn was sure that things were going to work out okay for both Towanda and him. He found ***Inspiring Hope!***

Each day as soon as he had endured the pain of the physical therapy session, he would motivate his wheel chair into Towanda's room. There he sat touching her arms, legs, shoulders, neck and face. As he brushed her hair, he would tell her that he couldn't wait until they could begin doing things together again. It had been 19 days and still no sign of any type of recognition or movement. Yet, Shawn was sure Towanda knew he was there and that she would not give up on life.

Shawn told us the next part of their story with such an exaggerated smile on his face that we knew it would certainly be inspiring to hear. It was the morning of day 20 following that fateful accident. The day was going to be filled with thunder, lighting and heavy rains, so Shawn intended to spend the entire day with Towanda. He knew that she had always been a little afraid when bad weather hit and he just wanted to be with her. As soon as he entered the room, he felt a change. He wasn't sure what, but he swears that he knew things were different. Over to Towanda's bed he rolled in his wheelchair and immediately took a hold of Towanda's left hand. He gave it a big squeeze and said he felt Towanda react. He was so excited that he hit the call button continually for anyone to come in to see. Then it happened. Her eye lids slowly started to open. He was sure of what he was seeing, but when the nurse came in, Towanda was still. Shawn began shouting at Towanda to open her eyes while continuing to gasp her hand as tightly as he could. Then the nurse got even more excited than Shawn as she went running down the hall to fetch a doctor. Towanda had moved her hand. Both of us saw it at the same time. It was really happening. Towanda was coming back to us.

Over the next two days, Towanda slowly came out of the blanket of darkness she had been in since that awful night when the drunk driver crossed the path of their lives. It took another three days before Towanda could return a kiss from Shawn. After four full years of physical therapy and speech therapy, Towanda has regained all of her functionality and swears to this day, that she pulled out of the darkness of her coma only because she felt Shawn there waiting for her. No one in the world could ever convince Shawn or Towanda that the power of touch was not the most important characteristic of their successful 31-year marriage and their lives together.

> As you can see from the power of touch that Shawn and Towanda experienced, the act of touching each other is a most effective and powerful form of marital communication bringing hope, love and joy. Even if your need for touching is not as great as Towanda's was, when you and your partner have practiced touching for awhile and get in the wondrous habit of touching, you'll discover just how marvelous this form of communication can be. And we ask you, how could you possibly spend even a minute angry with someone who just said, "I love you so much I simply must touch you."

From the hundreds of interviews with successfully married couples came the understanding that just as important as the act of touching is the underlying reason for the touching. They use touching as a substitute for language or a kind of **Morse Code** because they know nearly everything about each other. They have studied in infinite detail how their spouse looks, feels and acts. They know what makes them tick and can recite in scripture and verse their best qualities. They brag about each other all the time. Happily married couples are masters at completing each other's sentences. They understand their spouse's hot buttons, their cold buttons, their moods and what they are feeling in their heart. They communicate so much positive hope, love and joy with a simple touch. Making this an integral part of your marriage requires that your spouse becomes your favorite subject. Put the power of a loving touch into every part of your relationship.

It is our sincere hope that you and your spouse come to understand what our research says about the importance of touching in marital communication. But understanding and accepting the power and hope of this is only the beginning. You have to put the concept into routine practice before it will become a characteristic of your marriage. Once it does, you can feel the full power of a loving touch with its hope, joy and fulfillment. And yes, a loving touch has been known to have healing powers that go beyond anything that can be measured scientifically. Just ask Shawn and Towanda. They will never be convinced that they are not celebrating their 31st wedding anniversary together because of the power of a loving touch.

> **Twenty-five years of research on successful love and marriage has taught us many things, but first and foremost - no love has blossomed or been sustained without doing the "simple things." Big things don't matter until your relationship has mastered the art of doing the simple little things day in and day out in your relationship with another human being whom you purport to love.**

All too often in life, people make assumptions about love and relationships that do not stand up under scrutiny - that are not supported by the available evidence. So, what are the facts?

One of the great misconceptions of all time about love and relationships is this - just do the "big" things and everything will turn out well. And what do the Big Things include? For starters the list includes "having financial stability in your relationship," "being in love is all that matters," "having a good job and a house in the suburbs," and so it goes. But the truth is, these "Big Things" are important, but they are only a by-product of "doing the simple things." Here's what we mean.

It is an established fact - successful love is based on an accumulation of the "simple things." If you want your marriage and your relationship to succeed, just do the simple things! Do them day in and day out. When your relationship has mastered the "simple things" you have a chance to make it work. You have a chance to make it last. But if you don't, well, failure is an option.

There is another important fact of life when it comes to love and relationships - there will be big challenges to address in your relationships, of that you can be sure. You might have to deal with financial setbacks, serious illness, the loss of a job, or the death of a loved one. And trust us on this - if your relationship with the one you love has mastered the art of doing the simple things day in and day out, the likelihood of your relationship making it through the tough times are multiplied many times over.

The Loving Touch is one of those simple things. Give the one you love lots of daily hugs. Touch them often. Acknowledge their presence at every turn. Tell them you love them so much you must touch them. When the one you love is feeling blue, a simple touch can give them hope and a connection that makes all things possible. Remember what a loving touch did for Towanda and Shawn.

Simple things matter and when you practice doing them, they accumulate. Simple acts add up. You will be surprised at the power of your human touch. Start touching today.

What Would Happen If Today Was The Day That Changed Your Life?

By Katharine C. Giovanni

What if today was the day when your life changed for the better? If you look back, I'll bet my last dollar that you all can remember the one day that completely changed your life forever. That one day when your world tilted and it caused you to walk in a new direction. I can remember mine.

It was 1979 and I was 18 years old. I had just graduated from high school and decided to take a year off before I went to college. My dysfunctional childhood had turned me into an angry teenager with no direction. I was tired of being the family ping pong ball, and I wanted to get away from everyone.

So that summer, my father sent me away to a teen outward bound program. Mostly to get me out of the hot city, but I think he hoped that it might give me a new perspective on life. Since I had nothing better to do, I agreed and spent the next 3 months in the woods hiking up mountains, canoeing down rivers and generally learning how to survive in nature.

In the middle of the program, we were all required to spend three days alone in the woods. I was given a spot by a stream, a tent, and a small bag of granola. They checked on me a few times a day, but never spoke. They just walked by and waived.

The first thing I did was to hang my food up on a tree so the animals wouldn't get to it. Then I made sure that my tent was up correctly as I didn't want to get wet if it rained. Then, with nothing left to do, I started to think. I reached for the notebook and pen that I was allowed to bring with me and I began to write.

Soon, my brain took me back and I examined everything that had happened to me. The memories made me happy, sad, cheerful and angry. Back and forth it went as the memories flowed through my mind. Eventually, the garbage that I had been telling myself (and others) for years and years began to sound really stupid. It's hard to lie to yourself when you are alone with only your thoughts to keep you company.

By the end of the second day, I was finally able to see what I had become, and I didn't like her at all. She was a spoiled and angry teenager who was given a hard start in life certainly, but had a lot going for her in spite of it. I remember sitting under a tree and crying for hours. Then once I stopped feeling sorry for myself, I became angry and stomped around the woods throwing sticks and rocks and yelling at the air around me.

A few hours later, totally exhausted from the emotion of it all, I found myself on a large boulder by the stream where I had pitched my tent. I can remember watching the sun set behind the mountain I was next to, and then staring mindlessly at the fish in the stream. I poked at the water with a stick to pass the time. My mind was numb by now and I felt empty. I had nowhere to go and no one to talk to.

It was just about then that it happened. I'm 47 now and I can still remember the exact moment when my entire world changed.

As I stared at the water, a slow anger started to boil underneath my skin. It was as if something in my brain snapped. A fierce determination overtook me and I remember thinking that I would show them all that they were wrong about me. My family was an example of how to do it wrong. I decided right then and there that I would be an example of how to do it right, and I would help as many people as I could in the process.

Once the solo was over, I began helping out everywhere I could. I helped build the fires, carried as much in my pack as I could, and helped cook every meal. The counselors were stunned and asked me what had brought on the change. They told me that in all the years they had been leading kids in the woods, no one had changed as much as I did. I just shrugged and told them that I had simply decided to grow up.

Unfortunately it took another 15 years before I was finally able to become the teacher that I dreamed about on that rock so long ago. Why? Mostly because I was young and had a lot to learn, but I'll never forget the moment when it all started. I'll never forget that sunset and the way the light played with the water in the stream. As Oprah would say, it was my "ah ha" moment.

How about you? Can you remember the day that changed your life? What if today was another one? What if today was the day that you decided to be a lighthouse to the world and change your life? Why can't we just decide to make today the day? The day when our world changed into a positive, abundant, loving world? The day when we started to do what we actually wanted to do? The day that we started to live our destiny?

I think today is a good day to start. It's the perfect day to change your world. Take a deep breath and start walking toward your life's goal. It doesn't matter whether you take big steps or small, just take a step.

Since today is the first day of the rest of your life, why not make it the day that changed your life for the better—forever!?

Christ Our Hope

Dr. Thom A. Lisk

"... loves differently; the one who hopes has been granted the gift of new life" –Pope Benedict XVI, Spe. Salve 2

Above all, some would claim, hope is a theological virtue that has sustained the Church and her leaders for 2000 years. If it were not for hope we would not have a Christian Church, in any form, today. And, we would not have soldiers defending our country around the globe and here in our homeland if it were not for hope.

And, we may not have you or me! Think about it. **"Faith, hope and love, and the greatest of these is love"** we hear at many weddings, an expert from the reading of I Corinthians 13 in the New Testament of every Bible, whether Catholic, Protestant, or interested observer. You need not be a practicing Christian or even a Christian by baptism to love that verse about faith, hope and love.

It makes sense that "the greatest of these is love", and if you have studied love, you know it comes in all types. More love may help you to generate more hope in many situations in your life ahead. More of the right kind of love.

Jesus is Love personified; the best example of the best love. Sacrificial love is said to be agape or giving in nature and of course, the ultimate sacrifice in love is to lay down your life for another person. Jesus did that for all mankind. And, we see that kind of love in how soldiers gladly fight a cause they believe in as they willingly lay down their lives. They do so in hope in the cause, the country for whom they serve, for the people back home.

History is replete with stories of those who gave their lives in hope and for hope. Here are just a few:

War story of hope

A Catholic priest friend, well loved and respected in our central Ohio diocese, was mourned when he passed away to his eternal reward in heaven. Monsignor Joseph Maroon embodied, at least to me, what Christian people, especially pastors, are supposed to be…full of faith, hope and love. He was a veteran of the United States Army before finding his calling and went into the priesthood. Father Maroon retired at about age 70, being born in 1929, but was called back into service in some challenging situations. He brought hope to congregations that were exposed to bad priests, or at least priests that did enough wrong to be asked to leave the ministry. What makes one person strong to resist temptation and one succumbs?

Let's always remember we do live in a time of war, spiritual war, and the enemy of your becoming your best is not simply your own weak human nature, there is a devil who is out "to kill, steal and destroy" (John 10:10) But the good news is the rest of that same verse…"Jesus comes to give you life (and hope!) and give it to you abundantly."

You can win every battle you will face in life with patience and through closeness to God in a constant state of prayer. The "Good Book" says to "pray without ceasing", listen to the voice of God by the promptings of His Spirit working within you, and do what He says, then you will have Victory, you will win every war you face—although you may loose a few skirmishes. None of us are perfect!

Risk Tolerance

"Hope" and the word "should" are two of the most overused words we have heard the past year or more." This statement I heard on a CNBC from a financial commentator about the state of the economy. It may be true that we need more than hope to make money in a recession; we need the facts on our side. When investing in anything, wise investors look at the fundamentals and may do a complete technical analysis. Wise investors make decisions based on many factors, including their risk tolerance. You do not just hope for a return on the investment of your precious capital or retirement monies. You want a sure thing, or nearly so.

> **Risk tolerance says a lot about how you run your entire life when you think about it objectively.**

A Catholic priest like the one mentioned just above does not "count the cost" in what he gives up to be a celibate all his remaining life as he enters the seminary. He realizes he is giving up the opportunity to have a family and his own children, but he sees he will be getting far more than what he gives up. He lives in great hope.

Any minister has a high tolerance for risk, it seems to me, and yet he (or "she" in protestant churches) has hoped that "everything will work together for good..." They bring the best kind of hope to other people and are able to do so due to the abiding hope of Christ living within them.

Consider Please!

The following thoughts may seem random; even so they are important for any serious-minded person to consider.

Consider please...**If I do not hope in God I have a hard time hoping in YOU.** You need others to hope in you, don't you?!

Consider please...**How can I love my enemies if I can't love my friends?** The Holy Scripture says to love our enemies; first, we must "love your neighbor as yourself" only then can you love an enemy. And we all remember the rest of that new commandment? "Love God with all your heart, soul, and mind, and (then you can) love your neighbor as yourself." We are able to love others, hope in others, because we properly love God and ourselves, first and second.

Consider please...**People commit suicide because they give up hope.** Suicide is the ultimate outgrowth of a life with no hope. Hope is essential to life itself.

Consider please... **Mothers often abort their babies due to a lack of hope; they don't have enough hope that all will be okay with themselves if they give birth.** There has, since it became legal in 1973 in America, a national debate about the abortion issue. Consider whichever side you find yourself on today, that the women who abort, do so due to a lack of hope. It is a complex issue, but instills hope, and women find strength to carry the baby and offer the child for adoption, rather than the alternative that can haunt them for their entire lives.

Consider please...**God will take care of your future no matter what happens to you or around you—His love is that great!** Trust is not easy to generate for people at times due to having been disappointed (or worse) by other people, sometimes even their closest of family members. That is no reason to not trust God. Remember that God is perfect love. He loves you unconditionally. Return to Him and find out!

Consider please...**Taking a pledge that no one will ever leave your presence again without more hope. God wants you to be a carrier... and dispenser of His hope.** If you are willing to make this kind of pledge to our Creator, asking Him to create within you daily for the balance of your life a wonderful abiding hope, so much so that you have enough to always share with others. Do you want that kind of overflowing hope?

_____Sign here

Consider please... **Some people force themselves to do penance to make up for their mistakes, their sins, to correct their behavior once and for all.** Crush your pride, as an example, with a great hope through some kind of new actions in your life that force you to be and act in humility, the remedy to the root sin of all sins; pride.

Consider please... **In the scripture even the woman caught in adultery was given hope by Jesus as He forgave her, but of course also said was, "Go and sin no more."** She was about to be stoned to death by her accusers. Don't accuse yourself too harshly; we all are sinners in need of a savior —God is our defense attorney!

Consider please... **Look at yourself; take the log out of your own eye, before you attempt to find something wrong with someone else.** The truth often is that the reason we know something is wrong with someone else is because we either have done the same thing, or could in certain circumstances. Look at yourself and give yourself hopeful ways to improve. As you become your best, those around you will improve.

Consider please... **People do not need your condemnation; they need the love of God manifested through you.** And, that kind of love brings hope to hurting people.

Consider please... **A woman came to a Catholic Church with the license plate that read, "Goddess"; she admitted she needed true hope from a True God.** She went to confession she said for the first time in her life. No one is to be God in our lives except God. You are not some kind of god, so stop pretending that you are. Humility finds hope.

Consider please... **Virtue returns when you decide to admit your vices, and pray for a new start.** Pride is the deadliest of sins and can blind you to what is wrong with yourself. Pride can bring on all kinds of other bad actions, or just laziness, often another sinful vice.

Consider please... **Faith comes from your intellect; love is an act of your will; whereas hope may come due to memory.** You have heard it said, "Faith, hope, and love, and the greatest of these is love." Well, in your memory, consider the times you have felt the most loved in your life, and see if hope does not return. Anytime you are feeling discouraged or not hopeful, think about how much you have been loved at various times in your life, and you are very much loved right now by an all-knowing Creator. God wants to create more hope within you to live in His love.

Consider please... **A small molehill can become a mountain to the person who looks down rather than up and over.** You have it within you to become an overachiever or over comer. The outlook is always better when you have an up look.

Consider please... **Giving hope is one of the greatest gifts you can give, and it is a free gift**. Too often hope as a gift from another person, maybe a loved one, is under appreciated. If you have no hopeful people in your life, in other words miss the gift of hope for quite some time, and you will know it when a truly hopeful person affirms you. You will want more and more of their hopeful attitudes. We are often magnetized (Law of Attraction) towards hopeful people.

Consider please… **Be a carrier of hope and increase popularity!** Who doesn't want to be more popular? When I was a senior in High School I was voted Most Popular in my senior class. Why not work towards that in your world too by treating people how you want to be treated: hopeful.

Consider please… **Some people live in a state of denial. They deny one or more things, even reality itself. Hope is real, hope is vitally important to life itself.** Suicide says someone has given up all hope. There is always hope!

Consider please... **Hope only on a human level can be a little bit shaky.** Example? A mother says to her child, "I hope you clean the dishes!" You can hope but sometimes you need more than an expectation. You need to inspect what is expected and have or give specific goals for when you want what is hoped for to become a reality or completed. This is often a very important part of human hope. Divine hope is something bigger or better than mere hope on a human level.

Consider please… **Bob Hope was a wonderful comedian and entertainer who was so very popular because he easily made us laugh at ourselves and small things in life.** The right one liner delivered in the right way at the right time can bring hope, and it also can bring joy and laughter and take our thoughts off of problems, making them lighter.

Consider please... **To say you hope in most human beings is not the same as saying you hope in God.** Jesus was a human being, but He also was God, "I and the Father are One," He said. Jesus will never let you down. We let him down. Never forget that. Don't blame God or His Church for the people in the church that may disappoint you. Look to the one and only Head of the Christian Church, and you will not be disappointed. You will find eternal hope.

Romans 5:1-5 "Therefore, since we have been justified by faith, we have peace with God through our Lord Jesus Christ, through whom we have gained access[by faith] to this grace in which we stand, and **we boast in hope** of the glory of God. Not only that, but we even boast of our afflictions, knowing that affliction produces endurance. And endurance proven character, and proven character, hope, and hope does not disappoint, because the love of God has been poured out into our hearts through the holy Spirit that has been given to us."

Billy Graham is a great American Story. Now you can turn on the TV on a Sunday morning and find Mr. Graham's son broadcasting a program titled: My Hope. Billy was "raised up" to become the most effective evangelist of a generation taking the "hope of Jesus Christ to a hurting world". And, he would be the first to say, "God can also raise you up to do great things for God." Will you allow God to do so? Will you cooperate with His divine plan and His possibilities to be manifested through your life?

Or, will you stick to "the old" ways of looking at things? By God's Spirit we can all be made new in our inner person, and become "new creatures," and do many new and great things we would have never dreamed were possible.

My own story is a testimony to this last fact. I have seen a gradual progression of change in my life after 33 years as an adult Christian fully committed to Christ. Evidence is much more than my simple weekly church attendance. I have been used by God to speak to all kinds of groups worldwide; and I have helped other speakers do so too all due to my original commitment <u>to make a difference with my life for God</u>.

I am no Billy Graham, nor did I have a father whose shoes I could wear or follow-in; however I am making a difference, and can make a greater difference in the future. And so can you! Your life is every bit as important as the life of a Billy Graham, a Barak Obama, you name it.

> **Don't sell yourself short. You are important to God. You are a son or daughter of the King of all Kings: Jesus!**

Many people do sell themselves short; they have, in other words, very low expectations. Raise your sight. Here is another view to please consider that can change your life for the better. Stories change lives.

Today as I write this it is 2/28/09 and I sit on a lawn chair at the Ritz Carlton Hotel & Resort in Dana Pointe, California. Although I just read that in January, California's "unemployed reached 10.1% with many more who do not also collect unemployment," I find myself very hopeful as I look out from a cliff at the scenic Pacific Ocean on a clear sunny day with a temperature "nearly 10 degrees above normal." The beauty of the flowers, foliage, palm trees and lovely architecture surrounds me; again. I conclude everywhere how great and good is God!

His creation is Wonderful! Unfortunately many have polluted the world and affected the world in some negative ways, and many other men and women continue to create beauty. Let's focus on the beauty. To my left is an unusual white home with panoramic windows atop another lower hill where Benny Hinn, world-famous evangelist, is said to live. That home must be worth many millions. Back in the lobby: Father Frank Pavone, President of Priests for Life, and I run into each other at this Ritz. God is the hope of Hinn, Pavone and the Jewish couple I met with this morning at the Ritz.

The Jewish couple—Scott and Michelle Silverman—reflected for me on their story of 30 years of marriage and also Scott's earlier drug and alcohol addiction and how he found hope and victory. He didn't find Jesus Christ but none the less, Scott found hope from God and as a result, he has made a wonderful contribution to our society. Recently he was an international CNN Hero of the Week due to his non-profit work as Founder/Executive Director of Second Chance, Scott is one of America's foremost experts in prisoner release and recidivism. Find Scott at TerrificSpeakers.com!

Scott, through his organization, is giving hope to hundreds of homeless people who need to get back into a productive life. Out of his set backs, Scott has created a vehicle to provide hope to people through a wonderful sustainable non-profit 501(c)3 organization. What does this mean to you?

Look for MORE ways you can deliver hope. Affirm:
I am a carrier of hope to all I meet! Pray:

> God help me to meet more and more people each day, especially as their speaker, in every kind of setting, so that I can be one of your best and most in demand spokespersons for hopeful living. I will inspire people to live more hopeful lives, and I believe if they will hope in Christ, they will receive as a gift the reward of eternal life, use me God to bless people, I pray hopefully. Amen

(symbolic portrait of people at work)

Teaching Others & Staying Open to Learning

By Liz Cosline

The profession of teaching is amazing and something that each of us has benefited from during the years. I salute all teachers that choose this as a career. It is hard to measure how many students were helped and guided along the way. Often the appreciation for teachers comes long after graduation, if at all. Appreciate your inspiring teachers!

There is something that is good to keep in mind. No matter where or when, there is the opportunity: keep learning. When attending a seminar you have a great opportunity to take away more knowledge. When hearing a sermon, there is the possibility that a cord inside you may be struck with just what you need that day. Or what we sometimes forget, is that when we meet someone along the way, even if we have met the person before, there is always the chance for teaching and the chance for learning.

I look at people as vessels of information because each human sees things a little bit differently. Perhaps they have experienced different things, seen different things, or have tried a way that is a little easier than the way I know. Or maybe it will be I that can make something a little easier for someone that person. Sometimes when views are talked over in a discussion, it allows something to be thought of a little outside how it always was thought about before. This often can spring forth new ideas and get rethinking happening with ways of doing things better or new things altogether.

At some time or other we will all experience learning. This is something that should never stop happening. It would be great if we could find a way to have every one look at learning as the opportunity it really is or can be. In the same respect, everyone will at some time, also be a teacher that someone needs. Whether a parent is teaching a child, or a child is teaching a parent or another child, a coach is teaching a player, or when a speaker is addressing an audience, there is teaching happening, yes learning takes place.

> What also is so grand, is that hope teaches us to keep going. Hope allows us to dream. Hope helps us get through the hard times and continue on the path we are meant to take. Hope lets us see past our own limitations. And it shows us that we can get through the obstacles that may get in our way. Teachers bring we learners hope!

Teachers have hope for their students. Students need hope for the future. Parents have hope for their children. Speakers and teachers and we writers have hope that words will help others. People need hope for their lives—give it to them.

So there is another great teacher – the best teacher is Hope.

And, due to Hope you can keep learning and as a result your future is what you can dream it to become.

A Tall Florist Deliveryman
Without A License
Coach Z Rich Zvosec

When I first met Marcos Santos he was attending a junior college in Temple Terrace, Florida. A native of the hard scrabble slums of Rio DeJaneiro, he had only been in the United States for a couple of years. Let's just say his English was not the best, but he was a very likable kid with a great sense of humor and a big smile on his face all the time. I will never forget one of the first things he said to me. I asked him how his English class was going. He told me he was writing a report on "Magical" Johnson. I knew he would be a struggle academically, but he was 6-foot-9 and a good kid. However, due to his transfer status he would have to do some additional class work to be admitted into the University of North Florida. He fell under a unique UNF rule that stated a junior college transfer had to transfer 60 hours or it would revert back to high school grades, regardless of a grade point average in junior college. When Marcos committed, we explained to him that he needed to take a couple classes at the local junior college. We added that we would do what we could to help him.

That summer, he enrolled in sociology and photography at Florida Community College-Jacksonville (FCCJ). One of our other recruits, Aaron Nichols, was already in town, so they shared an apartment. Marcos was hired as the tallest deliveryman in LaMee Florist history. One drawback was that he didn't have a driver's license. Therefore, someone drove him to each location and he walked the flowers to the door. The feedback was always positive. He was just a beautiful person to be around. He was the type of kid who could light up a room, he had a gift for *Inspiring Hope!*

Everything went along well until I got a call in the middle of the night from his roommate, Aaron Nichols. He told me Marcos was on the side of his bed threatening to kill himself. I got in my car and rushed right over. Upon entering the apartment I spotted Marcos on the side of his bed with his head down. He explained if he didn't pass his classes he would have to go back to his poverty stricken neighborhood in Brazil. He said he would rather die than go back home a failure. He then pulled out a gun from under the bed he bought at a pawnshop. There were a few tense moments, but finally I convinced him to put away the gun. We talked and talked until the sun came up. I assured him I would get him through classes. Talk about pressure. Making a couple free throws was nothing compared to that challenge. From that point on we met four times a week in the Waffle House for breakfast and I tutored him in sociology. I don't know who was more relieved when he received a passing grade—him or I. He was officially admitted. He went on to graduate from the University of North Florida. And, in fact, wrote such a heart rendering essay on his CLAST Exam that he scored a perfect score. Upon his graduation he went to work for the Discovery Channel in South America and rose to the top of the Weather Channel. Ultimately, he became the President of the Weather Channel in South America. **I hoped for his success and was rewarded with great satisfaction due to the successes he had with his life as I placed my faith in him.**

Wanting to do more he came back to Jacksonville with his wife and started a school for young students. His life was tragically cut short in a motorcycle accident, but his legacy will live on. To this day he is one of my biggest success stories.

A playful challenge from an audience member helps bring to life the importance of searching for and developing your passion, whether in the face of skepticism, long periods of self-doubt and/or having to accept (even better, learn to play with and laugh at) your own flaws and foibles.

Discovering Your Passion through Humble Practice and Outrageous Play

Mark Gorkin (Stressdoc)

Setting the stage for the dramatic close of my Practice Safe Stress program with the Virginia Commonwealth University (VCU) School of Dentistry faculty and staff, I declared, "Find something you love to do, that you are truly passionate about. Some will find it at work, others will need to explore outside of work. And I believe you get the most mood elevation and sense of meaning when it's an activity that allows for genuine self-expression and that challenges you to keep practicing in order to develop your skills." I then asked the audience a rhetorical question: "Can you tell I enjoy being up here?" Why do I enjoy it so? Sure I love the attention, and I love being center stage. You know the old adage: 'Vanity thy name is Gorkin!'" After the laughter subsided, I explained the real reason: "I can bring more of myself as a speaker than just about anything else I do. With years of practice -- stumbling, falling yet getting up again and again -- I can be serious and silly, thoughtful and emotional, aggressive or poetic, larger than life or even an 'orchestra leader,' helping others bring out their best music. And I can be outrageous."

Now I immediately shifted into walking my "passionate" and "outrageous" talk, by putting on my Blues Brothers hat and black sunglasses and taking out a black tambourine, thereby revealing a secret identity: "I'm pioneering the field of psychologically humorous rap music and as a therapist calling it, of course, 'Shrink Rap' ™ Productions." Predictably, there's an audible groan from the audience. And my response: "Groan now. We'll see who has the last groan." (However, in my defense, years back, an African American friend upon hearing the lyrics said, "Oh, so you're into 'Aristocratic Rap.'")

I then explain that this is my Charlie Chaplin Maneuver. ("Alas, after I'm through you may need the Heimlich Maneuver.") The pioneering comedic film genius observed that, "The paradoxical thing about making comedy is that it is precisely the tragic which arouses the funny. We have to laugh due to our helplessness in the face of natural forces and in order not to go crazy." Naturally, I note that what the audience is "about to see and hear will give new meaning to the word 'tragic.' And as for not going 'crazy,' it's way too late for that. So buckle up your straightjackets…It's the 'Stress Doc's Stress Rap.'" And not only am I belting out the words but I'm prancing around the room while banging on the tambourine. Here are some sample lyrics:

When it comes to feelings do you stuff them inside?
Is tough John Wayne your emotional guide?
And it's not just men so proud and tight-lipped.
For every Rambo there seems to be a Rambette!…
Well the boss makes demands but gives little control
So you prey on chocolate and wish life were dull.
But office's desk's a mess, often skipping meals
Inside your car looks like a pocketbook on wheels!

At the onset of my "performance," people seem embarrassed for me; some are just sitting there wide-eyed with their mouths agape.

(Clearly I'm perpetuating a stereotype, notwithstanding Elvis Presley, John Travolta and Justin Timberlake: the rhythmically-challenged status of the white male!) However, my bravery if not my witticisms win them over. Often the group begins clapping their hands to my self-styled beat. Once the lyrics are completed the room erupts in applause. After waving off the feedback, my immediate response: "I've been doing this long enough...I know when an audience is applauding out of relief!" And then, "All this shows after twenty years off and on of all kinds of therapy -- from Jungian analysis to primal scream -- I have one singular accomplishment. Just one: Absolutely no appropriate sense of shame!"

Finally, as the laughter subsides, a woman in the audience ventures a comment, likely on other's minds: "Don't quit your day job!"

And my rejoinder is fairly predictable: "It's too late...This is my day job!"

But then I seize the moment: "You know I'm just up here having a ball. I'm not worried about what others are thinking, or whether they are judging me. I'm just doing it cause I love doing it. And I do feel good about the quality of my lyrics."

We had come full circle: Finding your passion and doing what you love to do. First, I underscored the real satisfaction in being able to laugh at my own flaws and foibles, especially when vividly recalling the many years being much more self-conscious and less self-assured as a speaker. Of course, it wasn't easy overcoming my self-consciousness rapping in public. More to the point, "it took awhile to feel comfortable making a fool of myself." There was at least as much blood, sweat and tears as there was joy while winding along the path of mastery as a speaker and "Shrink Rapper." However, it was definitely worth it. As the psychiatrist Ernst Kris observed: "What was once feared as is now mastered is laughed at." (And as the Stress Doc inverted: "What was once feared as is now laughed at is no longer a master!")

Now, with extensive practice and with the initial encouragement from those early audiences, I'm just fulfilling my destiny: "Have Stress? Will Travel: A Smart Mouth for Hire!" Obviously, my goal in life: "Being both a wise man <u>and</u> a *wise guy*!"

Hopefully, this vignette will inspire a search for your passion and a commitment to purposeful -- humbling and playful, if not outrageous -- practice. And with a bit of luck, these words just may encourage one and all to... **Practice Safe Stress!** *If you do you will be Inspiring Hope!*

Go Back to School and See the World

By Amy Drake

I had always dreamed of studying abroad. When I was in college the first time and a newlywed, my mother was diagnosed with terminal cancer and required a lot of care for the remainder of her life, two and a half years. As an only child it was a struggle to work and look after my mother, much less continue my education. So, I put my degree on hold.

Twelve years later my marriage ended and I decided to go back to school. I had taken a few classes over the years, mostly on recreational subjects like figure drawing and ceramics, but the time had come to study in earnest. I reassessed my career goals and began perusing college catalogues to find the right program. I was also an avid reader of travel magazines, dreaming of destinations far beyond the boarders of my home town. One day, I noticed an ad that changed my life: the University of Cambridge, U.K., was accepting applications for a summer study program. My adolescent dream of studying abroad merged with my desire for learning and I *knew* this program was for me!

I filled out the application and had a telephone interview with a liaison office in American. Every day for weeks I ran to the mailbox hoping and praying for a response. I thought in all likelihood that I would get a polite rejection, but I gave myself credit for applying for the program. Finally, out of impatience I called the liaison office for an update on my application and was told that I had been *accepted.* I believe I was meant to find that ad—I had received a small inheritance which covered the tuition and my friends helped me track down the books on the required reading list in the days before the internet. My dream of studying abroad came true and I excelled in the program. My success gave me the impetus to complete a B.A. when I returned home. I discovered ***Inspiring Hope!***

I have since gone on another study trip abroad; to Paris as a student in a graduate program in literature. My fiancé' at the time, Dr. Miles E. Drake, Jr. accompanied me to France and we are now happily married. He is tremendously supportive of my goals as I complete a master's degree at Ohio Dominican University. I am grateful for all of the support I have received and the opportunities I have had to fulfill my dreams. I believe it was divine intervention which led me along the way.

Authors note: How can we not believe in a God who offers us all such great Hope? We have nothing to worry about, nothing to get stressed about; the God of Hope offers us all peace. May His peace be with you always and may He intervene in your life to give you success.

Soar Like Eagles

Kathy Slamp, M.Ed.

Wishful thinking! How often do we hear those words? We say them often—and casually; but in truth, the words "wishful thinking" are hollow. They imply that whatever we are "wish-ing" for is out of our hands, and we're "wishing" for some hocus pocus genie to pop out of the bottle and make it all right—whatever it is.

I wasn't a girl who played with dolls; I collected them, but I seldom asked for one or played with the few I had. That was a good thing, because I was raised in Fairbanks, Alaska —far from any major shopping centers. What my missionary parents were able to purchase in the local stores was only the basics for our rather meager, but happy, life. One Christmas, though, I saw her; she was in the Sears catalogue, and the minute I saw that doll, I wanted her; I visualized myself playing with her; and I "hoped" for her to appear under the tree. In my childish heart, though, I knew it wasn't possible that the large doll that said "Ma Ma" when she was squeezed and had real lamb's wool hair could be mine. I was never a selfish child, but I still "hoped;" I knew that it was all "wishful thinking," but I still "hoped" for a miracle.

To my total surprise, on Christmas morning, the doll that I had hoped for was under the tree. How could this be? Even as an eight-year-old, I knew Santa didn't bring it. There was even a little guilt that I had hoped so loudly that Mom and Dad had sacrificed beyond their means to satisfy my hopes. I was an adult, though, before I learned the story of my parents' true sacrifice for that doll. They had ordered it from Sears, but it never came. On the shelves of the Northern Commercial Co. (the only place in town to shop), there was ONE of these dolls. On Christmas Eve, I later learned, my father went to NCC and purchased that doll for $25.00—equivalent to $250.00 in today's economy—and equivalent then to a month's salary. My hoping hadn't put that doll under the tree; my parents' love did it. Their actions made my hopes come to fruition. The world we live in is pretty "hopeless;" and hopelessness perpetrates a lot of "wishful thinking." A lot of "if onlys." If only I had a better job; if only my parents hadn't divorced; if only I got the lucky breaks, etc. The "if onlys" are empty energy sappers that produce nothing. But hope! Now that's another story! When the world is putting its hope in failing banks, and people who let them down, we have an anchor that is firm and secure. The prophet Isaiah said it best: "*...those who hope in the Lord will renew their strength; they will soar on wings like eagles; they will run and not grow weary; they will walk and not be faint.*" (Isaiah 40:31)

What are you hoping for? Put your trust in God, work hard, visualize it, and believe for a miracle, AND find and keep Inspiring Hope within yourself and in other people.

The Practice Of Hope

Brenda Shoshanna, Ph.D.

It's one thing to say, "Be hopeful, look to the bright side, there's reason to feel good, no matter how dark things seem." It's quite another to develop the unique and precious capacity to truly live each day in a positive, uplifted state of mind, no matter what is going on, and to be a source of hope for others. This takes practice. It is not a fleeting feeling, which comes and goes. True hope cannot be pasted over feelings of anxiety and despair.

In order to attain a truly hopeful state of being, in order for it to be solid and dependable, we must also be able to face the darkness, learn how to encounter all kinds of situations, accept all parts of ourselves, and take a larger view. Rather than hide from what is unpleasant, we then become empowered to see the truth of that which is presented to us, and become able to stay planted in what is most real and beneficial for all.

There's a beautiful poem that says, "The precious jewel we have lost, some say it is to the East of us, others to the West." (Rumi). This precious jewel is an enduring sense of well being and hope. But how have we lost it, and where can it be found? Most of us spend our lives searching to the East and West, looking outside ourselves for that which will bring this treasure to us, that which will take us home.

However, as we embark upon the Practice of Hope, we soon learn that this precious jewel is planted within. We have simply to stop our usual ways of living, sit down, turn around, look within, and make acquaintance with all that we are and have been given, and all that we are not. In this way we open our own treasure house and find the precious jewel of hope.

The Practice of Hope is extremely enjoyable. It takes us on a journey to that which is unique, unexpected, beneficial and which will bring endless joy. Step by step we learn to walk on the path that we have been looking for. Come with me on this journey, one step at a time, let's live and Practice Hope.

(supports our immigration policies)

Hopeful!? – Now Consider!

Dr. Thom-Terrific Lisk
President/CEO of PSBI & TerrificSpeakers.com

Hope! Everyone needs it and these days we need more hope than ever before, certainly you must agree! So, if you want to refocus your life for the better, come up to high ground where you can see things clearer, make better decisions, or simply gain some quick inspiration or renewed enthusiasm for life, this is it!
This book is for you!

Hope! It is easy to lose hope. You never want to lose hope, do you? If you do you might as well stop living. Hope is as vital to living as is a breathe of fresh air, which incidentally is also easy to take for granted.

Maybe you don't appreciate how vitally important hope is until you are nearly 90 years old like my saintly mother, Betty Lisk. When I spoke to her today (as I write this), a Saturday morning, it was I who was giving her hope more so than the other way around, which even now is often the case. She planted so much hope into my life and the lives of others, I think this must be why she reaps hope today.

You can be more hopeful simply by giving hope to others. PLEASE… Think about all those IMPORTANT PEOPLE in your circle of influence and the value gained to them and in your relationship when you share some HOPE. What is hope?

Let's not simply look up the dictionary definition of hope, let's go way beyond that! THINK about who has given you hope in your life, starting at an early age, and you will then begin to better understand what hope is, and how you can embody it and give it to others. You have nothing really more important in your daily life then to be...

HOPEFUL!

Maybe that really should be the title of this book, simply: Hopeful! We all can benefit from stories of people who are hopeful! Look around you and even begin to examine the news based on who seems more hopeful than the next person. You will see a difference! A positive difference maker!

Here are some examples for your inspiration:

"Win or lose, Sarah Palin, Governor of Alaska brought a great deal of hope to the sagging ratings of John McCain when she was announced as the Vice Presidential pick for the Republican ticket in late August 2008 the day after the conclusion of what most agree was the best Democratic Presidential Convention ever." **Barak Obama** himself must be a person of great hope to have risen as he did. It was his hope, more than anything, that inspired people to want to follow and vote him into office. Yes... Great leaders know they must embody hope—for some it seems to come naturally.

Average or middle class people love to be around people that exclaim a hopeful life. But they can not go to political rallies everyday of their life to get a shot of hope. They, just like you and I must learn how to find or if necessary: manufacture hope. Stories about hope can lift our spirits and we can all be and do more as a result. We will share some of those stories of hope with you soon enough…you can be more hopeful. You can have more good things due to hopeful attitudes. And, attitudes or thoughts determine actions.

Actions determine your habits, and habits determine your character, and character determines your destiny, I have told my audiences this for years, learn the lesson!

> **Change your thoughts or your attitudes and you can change your destiny. The #1 ingredient in the recipe for a better destiny, is hope.**

"Our Economy is in Danger" read the HUGE HEADLINES Thursday September 25, 2008 in the Columbus Dispatch, my hometown newspaper. Let's face it. The media has a way of destroying hope. My Dad was a journalist, I know of what I write. Thank God he was balanced by marrying an extremely positive woman, his high school sweetheart, who became an award winning teacher who brought hopefulness to kids for 35 years. She is going strong at age 90, whereas my father's attitudes, more than anything else, did him in at age 68.

> **Want to live longer? Want better health? Want more and better friendships and relationships? Get an overdose of HOPE and get it everyday habitually for 30 days, at least, so you can change your life for the better—guaranteed!**

How can I guarantee you hope will improve your life?

Well, really it is quite logical and analytical what will be shared, but it is also full of emotion. Get the facts, but also realize our emotions often drive us to action.

Solution! If someone has a problem they can best solve it with an attitude of hopefulness. Now, I am not talking about a Pollyanna pie in the sky kind of hopefulness. I am now talking about rubber meets the road real life hope based on facts. That is why stories can inspire us so, because if we read about someone who has overcome some great obstacle or difficulty in their lives, the inference is always, "if she did it so can I!" "If he did it so can I!"

Facts! People we admire most are those who have hopefully overcome great challenges in life. Every four years we have the Olympics -a several day event that captivates the entire world. Why? HOPE! What athlete starts out without a hope that they can't improve and do better, win more, score more, be better in a variety of ways!? If an athlete gives up hope, he or she gives up practice and soon they give up the possibility of participating, let alone competing to get a medal. We all know that simply participating is winning.

You need hope to participate in the game of life. "Never, never, never, never give up!!!" was the famous line delivered by Winston Churchill during the darkest days of WWII when many of the English people wanted to give up, throw in the white towel, surrender due to the relentless bombing of the Germans in and around London. Thank God history shows they kept hope when they were about to give up hope and surrender. It is always too soon to quit!

The last book I wrote, even though paid an advance by Penquin/USA, one of the largest publishers in the world, I found myself wanting to give up and quit several times, especially one particular day when things were going well. So, I went to a local bookstore, looked around for inspiration, not just at some books that made it to the shelves, but I also found a large $10.98 poster that I read and promptly purchased to see and read daily. It gave me hope to continue! It reads...

When life leaves you hanging… (Picture a white kitten hanging onto the end of a rope with claws dug in)…

DON'T QUIT!

Don't quit…(consider this the A—Z's of Winning!)

A…anything can happen.

B…Bend, don't break.

C…Challenge your potential.

D…Destiny is a choice.

E…Effort creates opportunities

F…Follow your intuition.

G…Get back up and try again.

H…Hold on to your vision

I…Impress yourself.

J…Just dig a little deeper.

K…Keep knocking on doors.

L…Learn from mistakes

M…Motivate with compassion.

N…Nothing worthwhile comes easy.

O…Own a positive attitude

P…Problems hold messages.

Q…Question what's not working.

R…Regroup when you need to.

S…Stand up for your principles.

T…Think outside the box.

U…Unite perseverance with resolve.

V…Value knowing when to walk away.

W…Work smarter, not just harder.

X…Xhaust all possibilities.

Y…You can, if you think you can.

Z…Zzzz's, take naps as needed.

Thanks to Meiji Stewart for writing the Don't Quit lines A-Z above. I wanted to place an exclamation mark after many of the A—Z, how about you? Today? Tomorrow? Yesterday is past. Let's set some new goals for the future, and start with better attitudes of mind and being much more HOPEFUL!

Hopefulness will not only change your life, it can change your family, your neighborhood, your city, your state, your nation, you entire world!

NOW! Get busy sharing hope! Share your story and the stories of hope in this book with people today! Inspiring!

Send me an email at… ThomLisk@TerrificSpeakers.com Help me bring hope to the world and change the world one person at the time for the better. **Submit your story!** If your stories are selected you can be in the next best selling book which this world desperately needs. Get busy today! Send me a note saying you want to be included in the next book. Also… you can phone me anytime at 614-841-1776: Dr. Thom A. Lisk

Now!

What brings you the most hope? Do you have mood swings? We all have mood swings however if your mood swings low, you need not stay in a low mood; you can move to the top floor.

Not long ago, I stayed in a five star hotel and while in the concierge lounge looking over a panoramic view of the area, I thought how truly fortunate I was, how truly blessed. I looked below, and to the right and left as far as the eye could see, and I saw both, signs of prosperity and also poverty. Within a short distance you could see great wealth displayed as well as great squalor. I said a prayer for those in need; and another prayer for the rich, that they would not just further enrich themselves but also reach out to the neediest among them. Then it dawned on me…

"What am I doing to help the neediest in my world?"

The more you study and compare and contrast those who have and those who have not, you realize thinking and hope changes people and circumstances. Now, we must realize that some people are truly victims of their environment or circumstances. I am not so much thinking of only America, I am thinking about poor areas of the world where hope is desperately needed, along with the basics for daily existence. We can take so much for granted!

Consider Norma Rudolph, born into near poverty, one of about 20 children. She contracted polio as a child and was told, "You will never walk!" let alone run. Run she did, winning a Gold Medal in an Olympic race, becoming at that time, the world's fastest woman. Thank God she has a mother who believed in her and never gave up on her potential.

Were you so blessed with a mother and/or father who believed in you? Regardless of whether you were or not it is not too late for YOU. You can find people who believe in you, who help bring hope into your life. For starters you may need to start giving hope to others. Plant the seeds if you expect a harvest. Personally, I have found some of the most hopeful people at various churches I have attended over the years. And, yes, I have found some "bittle-twiddles" too. What or who is a bittle-twiddle?

The story about one pastor who found "bittle twiddles" when he took over as a pastor of a well-established church is not uncommon. This positive hopeful man of God found people more concerned with the way things have always been done than with the possibilities of what could be. These kinds of people can defeat the best intentioned and best equipped people if you are not ready to persevere and furthermore understand human nature.

We are all too easily creatures of habit. And, some habits are good, some are bad, some are quite neutral. On a scale of 1—10 with habits being at 10 great and something that must not be changed, and 1 being a horrible habit that must be changed, let's ask ourselves about all areas of our lives. **"Which habits need improvement ASAP?"** Most people need a persuasive reason to change; and in truth we all need HOPE that making changes will be worthwhile, otherwise clinging to the status quo is the norm.

<u>Rate the following areas of your life 1—10</u>

Getting up in the morning fresh with one alarm sound ____

Reading something positive first thing in the morning __

Getting some morning stretches or exercise daily ____

Eating a healthy breakfast ____

Driving without stress to your work every day ____

Enjoying your work and taking time to enjoy people ____

Making your work fun and eliminating negatives ____

Out of debt or only having good debt that is no problem ____

Read or watch something positive uplifting at night ____

Being happy, thinking positive, going to bed on time ____

If you rated yourself in all ten above and gave yourself 100%... congratulations! I must meet you! You are the first perfect person I will have ever met! Are you objective about yourself? Maybe you need to allow someone else to rate you. If you are about 9 out of 10 on average on all above, you are still doing great! Or 7-8's too... terrific!

Regardless, develop an action plan to improve. Do you habitually choose from the "Terrific side of the menu or the terrible side of the menu?" as my friend, and speaker mentor Ed Foreman labels it? Let me tell you a small part of Ed's amazing story.

Mr. Ed (not the horse) is an inspiring example of what is possible when someone lives habitually in *Inspired Hope!*

Ed Foremen was the only person in the 20th century to be elected to the US Congress from two different states (TX and NM) and both before age 35. Before that, he became a millionaire business man where he discovered "Congress needs changing and by golly I am the man to do it."

I attended Ed Foreman's Executive Systems Successful Life Seminar –a three day life enhancing experience –and offer him from our Professional Speakers bureau. If we could all practice what he practices daily, the world would be a much better, more hopeful place. He reminded me why my mother gave me the nickname Thom-Terrific when I was a kid. Think Terrific, act terrific, and you will be terrific.

Now Consider!

<u>Now consider</u>… a young couple that is pregnant with their first child. What future mother and father are not filled with hope for their new child? To be otherwise, is certainly not what we could label "normal". I could mention several such couples I have known but I think in particular of Sarah & Todd Palin who learned while pregnant, that their fifth child had Down Syndrome and rather than abort the unborn child (not simply a fetus), they took the high road of hope to believe that all would be okay, somehow the special needs child would enrich their lives, never be a burden, only a blessing. Hope brought that new life into existence, and every new child born is a product of hope if you really analyze it.

<u>Now consider</u>…the seasoned man or woman who retires at age 65…Yes, after working for more than 40 years I think of several people I have known who have retired. Can you think of a few too? I have known people like Mike, who died within a week after retiring, and others, like my mother Betty, who at age 90, is still living a rich and rewarding life. Maybe you have gone to the retirement villages or rest homes to visit people like I have, and what did you find? Did you think about it much? Did you notice not simply that women out live men? But, what quality of life some people enjoy in their "golden years"? I tell you, the difference from a "grumpy old man" and a "glorious old girl," is hope!

<u>Now consider</u>…the young person who graduates from college… of course most new graduates are full of hope, or so you would think, right? Some few don't even go to the commencement exercises to hear the usual message of challenge for the future. I have spoken to both high school and college graduation exercises and have seen non-verbally those filled with hope, and those who are not. Establishing new goals at crossroads in our lives does take hope, a willingness to start over with enthusiasm and hope. You may have read about the Founders of Wendy's, Dave Thomas, who never received his high school diploma until he was in his 60's, well after he had made his fortune. I was at his funeral…those who know him, know him as a wise man with the equivalent of many college degrees, a man full of hope.

<u>Now consider</u>…the business woman or man who wants to start their own business…it could be you! Maybe you have read stories about people like Dave Thomas, just mentioned, and you believe and say to yourself, "If he can do it, so can I." Now, you need hope to find all the answers, but they are out there if you persevere and apply them. Thank God for entrepreneurs like Walt Disney who went bankrupt several times before he finally made it, and, boy, when he made it he made it BIG, you know what I mean?

Thankfully he kept his hope alive during all kinds of setbacks and defeats.

Now consider…the teacher who can share hope or give up hope and leave what some people call "the most noble profession—teaching." Originally, I wanted this book to be written by teachers or speakers with stories only about teachers. We have all had a few great teachers—at least I hope that is the case. I never had my mother as a teacher other than at home, however, I could tell you about several of my teachers from first grade through graduate school. Recently I saw one college professor from whom I took a Creative Writing class. Dr. Ashbrook is now a Dean at Capital University. He gave his all in that class, and I am sure in other classes too, hoping that they could be writers and be published. Few would work to do so later on I suppose, but still he delivered hope in how he spoke about the value of writing.

Now consider…the woman who is married to the same man for 50 years, who becomes more active after his death than before, and she goes on to live to age 100. My own wife was widowed after 19 years of marriage due to a sudden and unexpected heart attack of her first husband, a well-respected pediatrician. Initially, when she got the news she wanted to totally give up hope. Lorna said, "All I wanted to do was die too!" Somehow, she says by God's grace, she grew, lived stronger through the challenging times after becoming widowed, and stayed focus on getting better, never bitter. That is what Lorna did as she chose to focus on the many happy years of marriage together, rather than what she had lost. She was whole, healthy, and happy and a great joy to be around when I met her four years after as a widow. She gives me hope! She and I have met others that today do the same… live in hope.

Now consider…the Wall Street broker who makes money for all his clients, and as a result, he gets rich in the process. Or, you could consider the Wall Street broker that is greedy and looks out mostly for himself and he hurts rather than helps people. 75% of all brokers may not survive the recent deep recession.

<u>Now consider</u>…the blue collar worker who works in a manufacturing facility all his life as a member of a union and he eventually becomes a union chief. He looks out for all the other blue collar workers even though he now often wears a suit and a tie. He fights for his people and often their hope.

<u>Now consider</u>…the clergyman who at age 85 is not really retired, he keeps saying Mass and ministering to those in need six days a week. He seems to exude more love with each passing week; at least some who encounter him feel that way. What is his secret? He says, "It is Hope with a capital H. Jesus is my Hope, I have no fear of tomorrow because I know Who is in charge of all my tomorrows."

<u>Now consider…</u> the dieter who you have seen on TV, the one who lost 100 pounds in the past year. The before pictures make one wonder, "How could this be the same person!?" The one I think of is a woman, but men have accomplished the same dramatic results and they all do so with hope that it is possible! Often to accomplish such a BIG goal, they have more than some fancy new diet or exercise program or competition that drives them. They have a **vision** of the person they can become. If they stop living in hope, they can easily balloon up to their former weight again. Keep hope alive!

What do all these people have in common in these "Now consider" stories? That's right! They all had great hope! And you need hope not in a past tense, you need hope now!

Which of these people above can you most identify with? And, you will find others in this book that will provide you **keys to success by creating a more hopeful you.**

"Without a vision the people will perish." Proverbs from the Bible provides us many truths and much wisdom and can enkindle in us great hope; find the Master of Hope!

One Day

Diane F. Wyzga, RN, JD

Marketing posters hanging on the wall in my local bank read, "Someday I will [fill in the blank] have a home, own a business, etc. I keep meaning to tell them that they are sending the wrong message. But I get involved in my banking business and I forget to say anything. Until I go back into the bank.

What's my complaint abut the word 'someday'? It says that someone is only dreaming about the possibility - but not really expecting the possibility to come true. It's hope without the follow-up. Instead, if you really want something you would say, "One day..." As in "One day I will fall in love for real." You think that's a silly dream for a middle-aged woman living in sunny Southern California? Not so much. Sure, for the most part, men are looking for the same package: a 32 year old, doe-eyed, Size 2 woman driving a late model BMW, athletic, and fashionably dressed, pressed, and ready to go.

The last time I checked Size 2 was something my niece wore - when she was age 2. I'm fit but in a robust way, healthy and glowing. You wouldn't be able to shred a head of lettuce on my pelvic bones. My Volvo is clean, sporty, and has a kayak rack. And I am a lot more fun, independent, relaxed and more tolerant than I was at 32 years old.

Even so, after a number of years of being alone and on my own, I still haven't gotten used to the idea that this could be the end of the story. I am reminded of my hope for true love when I walk back into the bank. Standing in line I re-word those posters on the wall: "One day I'll be even healthier than I am today - so long as I keep up my exercise." "One day I really will be a stand up paddle-boarder - so long as I take my lessons and practice." "One day I'll fall in love for real - so long as I keep my eyes open and believe that he's looking for me as much as I'm looking for him."

And that's how it goes. We can hope all we want. Don't get me wrong. Hope is something that helps make the world go 'round. At the same time we have to believe in what we hope for so we can see it and do something to make it happen. That's where the bank posters have it all wrong. It's not 'someday' but 'one day'.

I am reminded of a cherished folk tale. A woman, her husband and his mother live together in a small cottage. The husband, a woodcutter, has little work - so they are poor. He and his wife have not been able to conceive children to begin a family. And the mother-in-law is ill. By and by while walking in a woods, the wife finds a magic stone that will grant one wish. What should she wish for? Work for her husband? Having children? Health for her mother-in-law? What would you ask for? How would you solve her problem?

The wife does more than hope - I believe that maybe her hope led her to the magic stone. But now she is on her own to make hope real. So here is what she says, "One day, I would like my mother-in-law to live long enough to see her grandchildren eating food off golden plates."

Now that's the difference between 'someday' and 'one day.' Maybe the bank doesn't get it - but I am sure you do: what we hope for becomes real when we declare it.

2AOK--Change the World and Change Yourself

Michael A. Schadek

When my wife and I lost our three year old daughter Macy to cancer in 1998, I thought my life was over—literally. Any glimmer of hope or promise of happiness seemed to be extinguished the day we buried her. For a time, I was mad at the world, mad at myself and mad at God. How could such a precious child so full of life and love be subjected to such a despicable disease? Neuroblastoma—a rare and deadly type of cancer—ravaged her body and robbed her of the pure joy of growing up and experiencing life. If something so terrible could happen to a beautiful child that never harmed another human or uttered an evil word, how could I be assured that anything good would ever blossom again in my life? Hope and faith seemed laughable. Life seemed random, meaningless and tragic.

Just as death had nearly extinguished hope, life and love brought hope back into focus. My wife and I were quickly blessed with the birth of two healthy and happy boys and slowly we rebuilt a life filled with joy, laughter and great expectation. It was the very act of having more children and taking a chance on the future which allowed us to get our lives back on track and to truly begin to live again. It wasn't an easy decision. What if we suffered the scourge of cancer again? What if some other tragedy befell us and robbed us permanently of any hope?

It was precisely this experience of losing my daughter which helped transform my life. It was Macy's death that helped illuminate a compelling and startlingly simple truth which has forever changed my life: life is about love, and love is actionable. It is how we treat others each and every day that determines our worth as individuals. Every day enables us the opportunity to help a family member, friend, neighbor or total stranger. By proactively engaging in positive acts of kindness, we make the world a better place and we make ourselves better people. Life is precious—we all know that. Time with those around us is literally passing before our eyes never to be recaptured. I only had 3 years with Macy, much of which was spent in a hospital watching her die before my eyes. In hindsight, I regret the myriad of moments when I didn't take action with her but sat by as a spectator. I regret the things I didn't do with her. I regret the things I didn't say to her. I regret the times I didn't hug and kiss her as if it would be the last day I saw her. Sadly the number of days I had with her were agonizingly short, and I regret most the acts of love I didn't perform.

My loss of Macy became the foundation of change in my life, and I will never be the same. I realized I could not longer sit idly by and watch the world pass by. I had to take action and become part of the solution rather than part of the problem. In an age of terrorist attacks, economic meltdown, increasing crime and rising depression, I could no longer afford the luxury of retreating into personal ambivalence and apathy. I tried that after Macy's death and it didn't work. My sadness and pain and depression didn't abate by burying my head in the sand. I needed to take action and take control of my life. I did this by developing a simple process that everyone—regardless of age, financial werewithal or intelligence   can put into effect IMMEDIATELY.

Two Acts of Kindness—2AOK for short—is a lifestyle commitment that literally changes your life—and the world—

from the moment you begin the system. The requirement is ridiculously simple: commit, beginning TODAY, to perform two acts of kindness each day for the rest of the year. Some acts will be large, some will be small. Some will take preparation and planning, some will occur in the blink of an eye. Some acts will take place in public, some will take place in the silence of your heart. All, however, will be priceless because you will be making an empirical difference in the lives of those around you. But for those two acts of kindness each day, the world would not be better off. Because of those two acts of kindness each day, not only have you elevated those around you and literally "made things better" but you have also increased your significance and meaning in the world. You truly matter and your acts serve to elevate not only those around you, but you yourself are elevated to a more meaningful role. By helping others you help yourself. As Mother Teresa instructed: "Do not wait for leaders; do it alone, person to person."

The second requirement for 2AOK is to record your two acts of kindness each day in a journal entitled The Kindness Vault. The Kindness Vault serves a dual role. First it encourages accountability for your actions. You must take the time to record your two acts each day and this requires forethought on your part. Secondly, and more importantly, The Kindness Vault serves as a tangible and daily reminder of the positive impact you are making each day. You now have concrete and empirical evidence of the difference you are making in the world. These acts can never be taken away and no matter what happens in your life, you have a treasure trove of acts which are truly priceless. The contents of The Kindness Vault will eclipse the contents of your bank account in true value.

You and I CAN change the world, two acts a day. Your acts may include volunteer work at a local charity or it may be a simple smile or kind word to a stranger. It may be a phone call to a lonely neighbor or the gift of time for a family member. It can literally be anything, but you must commit at least two every day and you must record them in The Kindness Vault. If you do this, your life will change dramatically and the world around you will change. As Marian Wright Edelman succinctly stated, "A lot of people are waiting for Martin Luther King or Mahatma Gandhi to come back—but they are gone. We are it. It is up to us. It is up to you." 2AOK serves as a roadmap to put this conviction into practice. In the end, 2AOK restores hope to each of us and promises hope to the world. I only wish Macy was here to participate. How I would love to watch her two acts of kindness each day.

(nature interacting with historical landmark)

From the special commemorative section of the Columbus Dispatch with news about the inauguration of the 44th president of the United States:

KINDERED SPIRITS? The nations first African-American president said on January 18th that "Together, we can carry forward as one nation and one people, the legacy of our forefathers that we celebrate today." Two days later, Barack Obama took the presidential oath with a hand on the Bible used in 1861 by **President Abraham Lincoln.**

Mr. Obama said at his swearing in: "I stand here today as **HOPEFUL** as ever that the United States of America will endure-That it will prevail, that the dream of our founders will live on in our time...never forget that the true character of our nation is revealed not during times of comfort and ease, but by the right we do when the moment is hard." **Barack Obama--**44th *president of the United States of America, in a speech at the Lincoln Memorial on the eve of his inauguration.* A special note from the **Author Thom Lisk**: Is it ever right to abort a baby? No! 44 million babies have been legally killed in America; that is not right Mr. Obama! It is hard to change our minds, change our positions politically or otherwise. Mr. Obama shows his true character by supporting abortion a position that does not bring *Inspiring HOPE!* Get the facts! Vote pro-life which brings more hope to America and the world! God will bless America more if we outlaw abortion. Abe Lincoln had to be pro-life and that Bible upon which Mr. Obama took his oath is a pro-life book! If Mr. Obama remains pro-choice he is breaking his oath. Pray: God help us all keep our promises!

More Hope Creates More Motivation!

Dr. Thom A. Lisk

Everyone needs motivation on an ongoing basis, and some days it is more challenging to be and stay motivated than others, you know that, right? In this chapter, for sure you will learn some things you do not know, that will get you motivated, keep you motivated, and help you to motivate others. Do you understand the great value to being much more motivated day in and day out?

The most exciting way to live, is in a constant state of motivation and it could be—think deeply about it—that true HOPE is the root cause or seed that can germinate into outstanding motivation... so that you reach your greatest goals. You need to follow some steps, I have discovered (and now document) the hard way after 40 years in the work world. This is an IMPORTANT chapter in this book... maybe the most important material you will read this year or any year! Highlight what you read in this chapter!

Don't forget what you read in this chapter! Apply what you read in this chapter and I can promise YOU a much brighter, happier, more successful future! Do you want that!?

YES! **Regardless of what the uninformed skeptics think or say, EVERYONE NEEDS MOTIVATION. What is motivation anyway?**

You know of various types of motivation. Does that mean there are different kinds of hope too? Discover the answers so that you can propel yourself to more success.

Success comes from serving, serving others better.

Notice I did not write, serving others better than someone else. That may not necessarily be a motivation of yours, at least in your top ten. Some people actually claim they are not interested in success. In my experience and research, it is because of how they define success. Words are wonderful things and certainly do connote different things for different people… words can motivate each person differently, and the same words may not motivate one, but do motivate another person. Keep reading please.

I want to be clear with the choice of words so as to bring you to the root of your motivation, so that you accelerate your success. To do so, it has been proven that sharing stories, especially personal stories, is often most motivational. We gain insights through hearing stories about real people, real lives, real circumstances; and we all know our own life story best.

Learn all you can through life stories. Let these words and stories feed your inner motivations to the core: you gain more hope!

Crossroad Hope

I recall, again, my early marriage at age 18—an elopement—and being a father at age 19. Had I not been filled with a confident hope how could I have survived let alone succeeded these past 40 years?! I actually had $10 to my name when I returned from our secret trip to Michigan in August 1968. That was a tumultuous year. We can not allow all the uncertainty in the world or economic challenges or other people's lives to shape our decisions—this was the right thing to do for me and my girlfriend. And Todd, now at age 40 has a great marriage and child of his own!

You may be at a crossroad in your life. Possibly the most good news is that God can bring good out of bad decisions in your life.

> **God is in control when you may not even be thinking about God or factoring in doing His will in your decisions. The God I serve and know can turn any lemon into delicious lemonade. He's done it for me, He can do it for you too!**

When I was in high school, some of my male friends did not like the rules of the Varsity Basketball Coach. In my case, the only rebellion I exhibited was a desire to not cut my hair to the coach's specifications. So in both my junior and senior year, I did not play varsity ball, rather I played in another organized league: Hi-Y Basketball played at the YMCA. We had a team from our high school just as others did. When I was a senior our varsity team was last place in their league, however, my team was #1 and I was the leading scorer on the team and in the league. Champs! #1!

Now in the past 40 years, I have learned many lessons that confirm that it is okay to stand-up for what you believe in. You need not go along with the crowd, simply being a person with a herd mentality. Hope that you can be someone uniquely better and different, and you can.

You need not rebel against the establishment or the way things have always been done, however, chances are that if you keep doing what you have been doing, you will keep getting what you have been getting. So, we must ask some difficult questions and act accordingly.

In sharing personal and true stories, I am hoping they trigger within you a hopeful attitude that brings about better actions, better habits, maybe even a better character manifested from you, and this, <u>I promise</u> can change your destiny for the better too.

For years I went to church by myself along with my two young children when that first wife of mine stubbornly refused to go with me. Week after week, year after year, it was hard on me to see other complete and loving so-called nuclear traditional families sitting together in church. Finally when Lynda began to go, one minister's message hit her the wrong way when it came to her from Romans 12:1, and the next week she filed for divorce. That was a tough time!

I needed hope to make it through those months, not just motivation. I would have done anything for my family and my wife, and now she was rejecting me because I chose to put God first in my life with only one evidence of that, my faithful and regular church attendance. "You've changed!" Yes, that was true and I had changed for the better.

Sometimes, people will not be able to accept you when you change for the better; change for the better anyway!

In life it is too easy to get bitter rather than better, but in writing this I am hoping to help you get better. <u>Never get bitter</u>. If you are bitter in some ways now, I want to help you <u>get over your bitterness forever.</u>

I know it is difficult. Things that happen in life, mere circumstances themselves, can trigger bitter thoughts and feelings. However, it is always best to forgive and do your best to forget. Start over with new hopes, new goals. Yes, you can if you think you can. "With God all things are possible!"

From late 2007 to early 2009, like nearly everyone else, I lost money in the stock market with my retirement investments, etc. Do I choose to get bitter about this or better? Invest better next time, hoping of course there is a next time. Thank God we always can have another chance till the day we die. Hope and plan to do better next time.

It is not too late if you can still read this to make things right with other people. Write a letter, send a card, make a phone call, and reconcile relationships to the best of your ability to do so. Don't burn bridges you may need that link later in life if you are fortunate enough to be here later. Count your blessings today. You will be much more likely to have more to count tomorrow.

Some of what I just wrote sounds like clichés to some of you possibly; however good advise is always worth repeating or reviewing over and over again until it is second nature.

Crossroads? We read in the newspapers or see on TV or via the internet news about lay-offs, some so massive that one company may be laying off several thousand people in their world-wide operations. Millions are unemployed, some for the first time and they don't know how to cope, how to hope for a bright tomorrow. Don't worry there is always Hope.

Forty Plus is the name of an organization helping people in transition. I have spoken to this organization on many occasions over the past 26 years. I have met people at career or work crossroads and worked to bring them hope.

In my case, when I was nearly 40, like with many people, I felt I had not accomplished much of what I could have yet in my life. I knew I needed to refocus, rededicate myself, maybe get more education, and acquire new vision, mission, purpose and more motivation. The solution I came to was a one year working sabbatical moving from Ohio to California, living nine of those months at a Christian seminary where I worked on two books, one of which served as a dissertation for an earned and honorary doctorate degree. It was a huge sacrifice and change in my life, but in retrospect well worth the change. If you were to consider something similar, make certain you prepare yourself and your family well in advance. Many marriages can not survive that kind of change. It was not a mid-life crisis in my case; rather a re-sharpening of my axe or skills.

Abe Lincoln once wrote, "The woodcutter who stops to sharpen his axe will cut the most wood." Think about it!

It is true, that after I returned to Ohio, even though in many ways I was starting over from scratch (again), my effectiveness was so much sharper. My decision making was so much better, that success was inevitable. As one friend put it to me one Monday morning recently, "The fruit of your efforts is visible for all to see even if most people do not know you are the Founder of what is now called the Catholic Men's Ministry, Diocese of Columbus. Thousands of men are the better for what you began" and this is only one of the things I began after my one year working sabbatical.

I emphasize the word "working" when describing my sabbatical because even though my environment changed and so did the kind of work I was doing, in large part it took a great deal of humility to make a great many changes in my life. I was motivated as I knew what was possible. I had a vision of the man I wanted to be, yes, and purpose to make a difference with my life which made every sacrifice worth it. Consider please…

You don't know anyone who has done successfully many of the things I have done, by God's grace. Like what? When I knew it was right and God's will for me to go to California, first, I sent out some letters to organizations that might hire me as a consultant so I could have some kind of income so as to not be a burden to my family who was to move out to California too once I got established—this seemed like the right plan at the time. As time went on, that plan changed and I returned to Ohio. But had I not stepped out by faith <u>in hope,</u> the many good things that happened to me from age 40 to age 59 would not have been possible. Think about:

Driving over 2500 miles in about two days! Is that possible? Yes. After dropping off my daughter Erin at her high school at about 7:30 am in Columbus, Ohio on a cold winter day with my car packed to the edges, I began driving. By the time I stopped that day, I had traveled 1050 miles in my Toyota Camry, and then stopped at a Church, where I slept for about six hours before resuming the trip the next morning, a Saturday. That day, stopping to jog for 5-10 minutes numerous times so as to stay alert and energized while also listening to motivational and educational tapes as I drove, I traveled 1100+ miles, leaving me in the high country west of Los Angeles about 250 miles. I fell asleep at a rest area in my auto so that no time would be lost. I resumed the next day Sunday morning at six am. As I exulted in the sunrise, I approached LA and then Orange County (just south of LA) where I arrived in the parking lot of the world-famous Crystal Cathedral with pastor Robert H. Schuller, my friend then, just in time for the 9am church service, which can be listened to in your auto.

Wow! After the church service was complete, I drove further south to my final destination that day in San Diego where my aunt Helen, age 83, lived with her husband Stewart. They had invited me to stay with them a few days until I got my bearings and my work was established. Little did we know what the future might hold but we had great hope.

At that time, I was a very devoted Protestant Christian. I had thought and prayed about becoming an ordained Minister. The timing never seemed quite right. Regardless, I was very involved in serving and living out my Christian life wherever I was led, having held several state-wide leadership positions in Ohio before age 40 in the church, and also as a business executive, professional speaker, consultant, and seminar leader.

My faith had helped to cultivate a willingness to adapt and change, and commitments to be a servant leader first and foremost. This commitment would find me enrolled at a seminary shortly after arriving in the San Diego area and living in a dormitory situation for nine months at age 40 while working night and day in a variety of meaningful ways. The evenings and weekends found me continuing my education (be a life-long learned) while working on two books, one became a national best seller, and the other served as my dissertation for the doctorate degree that Southern California Seminary bestowed upon me.

> **It would never have happened had I not hoped towards the vision that I could receive a doctorate, and act in faith accordingly. You must have faith, and act on your faith.**

"What really is important?" Pulitzer price winning photographer Jerry Gay called me recently in 2009, nearly 20 years after I left for my first major life sabbatical in 1990 echoing some of my current thoughts written here, as if to confirm that I was on the right track right now again.

> Have you had those kinds of confirmations? We want to provide signposts for your success direction in this book.

Jerry Gay is a visionary who talks about God the Father in such an intimate way, that you can better understand how God's love is reflected in all of life, and certainly is through his photographs and accompanying words. The lessons learned in life must be reflected upon so that we can share them with others. This is the essence of what I heard from Jerry by phone that eventful blessed Monday morning.

TGIM! Thank God it's Monday! Have you seen any t-shirts sporting that affirmation? I was in the grocery store and saw in the frozen food section, products from the TGIF restaurant chain. "Thank God It's Friday" is a cute way (but loser's way) to live life, in my experience.

Everyday is a day to be thankful to God! Yes, we are thankful when Friday comes most usually because we get a time of personal rest or personal focus. If you hate your Monday to Friday work, do get another job before it's too late; and in the meantime, look for motivation to find happiness and hope in every day. I bet the founder and owners of the TGIF sure are glad to capitalize on so many peoples obsession with the end of the normal work week.

As Zig Ziglar used to say, "Let's not call the weekend weak any longer, let's call it what it really is for most people, the strong end to the week or the strongend." How you label things in life can motivate or de-motivate, bring hope or diminished hope.

Motivation is defined by Webster's as "that within an individual that excites" or propels one forward. Tap that hope within you –get and stay motivated! Yes, you can if you think you can! Write down your hopes!—don't loose them.

May everyday forward be like Easter Sunday for you as your days will be full of resurrection and victorious life.

May you stay motivated and stay connected to True Hope to the day you die; and may you be blessed to go to heaven the paradise where hope is no longer needed, yes, you will no longer need hope. In this life you will always need all the empowering Hope you can be gifted with, by the grace of God. After all, everything is a gift from God including: Hope. God bless you richly.

We're Where We're Supposed To Be -
Once We Stop, Look, Listen For Signs

Dr. Susan Murphy

It was the fall and my life was filled with chaos and fatigue. I was involved in building a medical center with constant demands from the corporate office, colleagues, employees and physicians. I had a busy social life, busy community service life, and was desperate to find some peace. It felt as if I were serving as a gas station open 24 hours a day / 7 days a week where everyone could pull up to me when their gas tanks were on "empty" and get "filled up" with my energy. My own gas tank was empty.

It was time for a retreat - one where I could become centered and nurture my spirit. There was a retreat house about an hour from my home, so I registered for a weekend retreat - three days and two nights. I couldn't wait.

Once at the retreat house, I discovered I was to have a roommate. Darn, I didn't ask enough questions before registering! A roommate wasn't what I needed - but I thought, "OK, I'll be pleasant to this roommate, but there will still be lots of time for peace, quiet, and solitude."

I walked in silence to my room, took a deep breath, put my key in the lock, and opened it. My roommate had not yet arrived.

Within 5 minutes, my roommate burst into the room with "Hi, I'm Cheryl. We're going to have a great time this weekend!" For 3 days and 2 nights, Cheryl kept talking and talking, barely taking a breath between sentences. No wonder she complained of a headache. She shadowed me wherever I wandered on the beautiful rose-covered grounds. Cheryl was getting a divorce and she had 2 kids, one with Down's syndrome. She sobbed and cried desperately.

My heart went out to her... but I needed some relief too! Didn't God understand that?

The retreat ended on Sunday evening and I returned home - un-rested, un-nurtured, un-centered, and even more stressed than before I left.

Three days later, Cheryl called my office at the medical center. "I have a malignant brain tumor" she blurted out when I picked up the phone. She went on to say, "I feel so close to you," and thanked me over and over for my kindness at the retreat.

I was sad and ashamed. My behavior may have been kind, but my thoughts certainly had not. Suddenly it all made sense - her headache, her lack of control, her fear, her tears, her clinginess... plus, why I was supposed to be at that retreat on that weekend. It was for Cheryl. And it was for me.

Although my life continued to be chaotic, my own "stuff" didn't seem nearly so awful nor overwhelming.

I called Cheryl twice a week after that - just a 5 minute call - for about a year. Then she told me that her treatments were over and she was much better. I stopped calling... and stopped thinking about her.

One evening in the fall about two years later, I was having dinner with a friend at a restaurant. A lovely woman came to our table and asked me if I was Susan. When I said "yes", she came over to me, hugged me tightly and said "I'm Cheryl. I'm cured, I'm alive and I'm happy... and you are the angel who helped me. Thank you."

I'm convinced it wasn't a coincidence that Cheryl was assigned to my room that weekend at that retreat. I was recruited as an unwilling volunteer "angel" to help Cheryl through a terrifying, painful and lonely ordeal. But the more I think about Cheryl, the more I realize how much I benefitted from befriending her. It opened my heart, helped me put my own problems in perspective, and reminded me that everyone I come in contact with needs love and compassion, and hope.

Oftentimes, when we're chosen to be the "angel", we receive more than the person we're helping. I believe...

We're where we're supposed to be - once we stop, look and listen for the signs. So... Be hopeful all the time!

Second Sight
by Dr. Steven A. Vladem

> "Your son is rapidly losing his eyesight. His eyes are becoming cone shaped. With this physical defect, he will become totally blind in a short period of time. Do not plan to spend huge sums of money on him for an Ivy League education. He will never be able to complete his studies. Put your faith and hopes and dreams in your other children. There is no way that this son will ever be able to live a normal life."

As my doctor said these words to my mother shortly after my seventeenth birthday, she silently wept. I hugged her and whispered to her that I would somehow try to make her proud of me.

As a child, I was a shy and introverted bookworm, and, having extremely poor eyesight, I was a terrible athlete. I was always at the top of my class academically. I had the IQ of a genius and an unbelievably great memory. Everyone expected for me to become a skilled surgeon who would be well respected in the local community.

After hearing the horrible news from the doctor, we went to countless other ophthalmologists who repeated the same grim prognosis. We did find a doctor who developed unusual therapeutic contact lenses which pressed against the eyes and reshaped the corneas to the normal spherical shape. I had to endure extremely intense physical pain and suffering in order to try to achieve my goals. The doctors all said that I experienced the greatest pain known to man. In order to ensure that I would have decent eyesight, I had to see this eye specialist on a daily basis. Since he was located in Chicago, I had to go to a local university and commute back and forth to the eye specialist's office for treatment. (This was the only doctor in the United States who could possibly help me with my rare eye ailment.)

While taking chemistry laboratory classes in the premed curriculum, my eyes would turn bright red and I endured a great deal of pain and suffering whenever I came in contact with chemicals. I realized that I would never be able to fulfill my dreams of becoming an outstanding surgeon and I would never be able to save lives. I felt as if a curse was put on me.

I had a natural aptitude for working with numbers, so I studied mathematics, which did not require a great deal of reading and limited the strain on my eyes. I taught gifted students in high school by day, while taking classes in graduate school at night for advanced degrees in mathematics, educational administration and supervision, and computer science. I developed unique ideas for using the computer as a teaching tool and received worldwide recognition. I was honored at Oxford and Cambridge Universities. At the height of all my success, my world came crashing down on me. One of my eyes had ruptured. Gobs of white fluid covered my left eye and rolled down my cheek. I was in desperate need of a transplant. I had a very unusual tissue structure and the doctors were not able to find a suitable donor. I waited for months with a patch on my eye. Miraculously, they found a donor. A 33 year old woman from Michigan had choked to death while eating a sandwich.

Her family had approved donating her body parts for transplantation, and her eye was flown in to Chicago. The transplantation was successful. However, eleven months later, I experienced transplant rejection episodes and had to have six additional surgeries because of medical complications. After waiting more than a year and a half for a second transplant (no eye was available in any eye bank in the United States which matched my unusual tissue structure), I experienced a second miracle. A cornea became available from a high school freshman who lived sixty miles away from me. He was planning to become an engineer. On a late Friday autumn afternoon, he was rollerblading with his friend on an isolated country road. Darkness set in. In order to avoid hitting his friend, the driver of a van swerved and hit him. His head hit the pavement and he was declared brain dead. His parents decided to donate his body parts and I was given a second chance once again. I was given a second chance. I received his cornea a few days later. His tissue structure matched mine perfectly. It was like finding a needle in a haystack.

Seemingly by coincidence, opportunities began to present themselves where I felt that I had found my divine purpose in life. I became aware that transplant procurement centers and eye banks were only available at the time, in only nine countries in the world. If I had been born in another country and with a different set of circumstances, I might not have had the good fortune for a second chance. I came up with the unusual idea of transforming a one story building in Ramat Gan, Israel, which was being used as a blood bank, to a five story "house of life" containing a blood bank, eye bank, and a transplant procurement center. Although my ideas for the project initially met with a great deal of opposition, I persisted, and miraculously, attitudes changed. I used this idea of a prototype of a "house of life" which would be replicated in countries all over the world, in Russia, China, Japan, India, Africa, Brazil, just to name a few. This would result in saving millions of lives. I am planning to work with the United Nations World Health Organization, and numerous Red Cross organizations from a wide variety of countries to make this happen. I became a motivational speaker and helped many people with handicaps and disabilities while promoting transplant awareness. I received a number of knighthoods and had the pleasure of having my parents watch the investiture ceremonies. I received the Science and Peace Medal from the Albert Schweitzer Institute. I was honored by the London Diplomatic Academy and received an International Peace Prize for daring to soar and create a harmony of mankind. I participated at an international conference at the School of Medicine in Madrid, Spain, and I received the DaVinci Diamond Award for being an innovator and a renaissance man. Many people tell me that I am one step away from receiving the Nobel Prize.

Numerous book publishers, literary agents, playwrights, movie producers, and Hollywood studio executives have shown a great interest in my life story. Never in my wildest dreams did I ever believe that all of these wonderful opportunities would become possible. Who would ever imagine that the roadblocks in my life journey would turn into wonderful opportunities? **At first sight, I felt cursed and could not understand why I had to endure such difficult circumstances. But, on second sight, I realized that these difficult circumstances presented me with the greatest *Inspired Hope* that I could ever imagine.**

Ultimate Hope

Dr. Thom A. Lisk

Now, let's consider ultimate hope in a deeper bright light of what the Mother Church has taught for nearly 2000 years. You may be more interested, however, in your own experience the last two, twenty, two hundred or two thousand days so that you make better decisions in the present, shaping a brighter future. Or is your ultimate destiny your larger more important concern?

Historians supposedly present the facts as stories of the past in their fullness. But such is really not the case, as time and space limit us all. Consider, please what good is history if it does not provide lessons for shaping a better future? **History that does not create hope is very boring most of the time.** Example?

If your history with eating is rather boring, you may not be hopeful about a fine cuisine presented at the best of restaurants. You have not been conditioned to be hopeful about your next meal. However, just start enjoying your next meal with more appreciation, a new understanding and slowness, and: Wow! Meals in the future become more a thing to hope for, more of an enjoyment, a true blessing.

We are ordinarily practical people, for the most part, concerned with things like food, shelter and clothing much of the time; maybe too much of the time? As we mature and progress in our life journey, we proceed up Maslow's Pyramid of Needs to self-actualization. This is a concern for ones legacy, in simple terms. How will I be remembered?

My story may be like yours in many ways, and I like you, prefer to focus mostly on the good things God has brought me in my life, and ordinarily only repeat the positive good things that have happened. I would now like to share some of my story that has not been written so you also learn more about the delivery of ultimate hope.

What would you do different with your life if you could live it over again? Review your life to day as you read...

Let's say you start with the day of your high school graduation. In my case I would do many things different. I might go into the ordained ministry, preferably Catholic, as I understand the full Truth now at nearly age 60. I am very thankful for my son Todd, now 40, who was a result of my celebration in the back seat of the auto with my girl friend, Lynda, the night of my high school graduation. (Be careful how you celebrate!)

One "mistake" or "sin" can change your life and destiny forever. I am very glad abortion was not an option. God can turn any "mistake"—a child is clearly never a "mistake"—into a great blessing.

Always... be patient, wait, hope, pray.

My life story is a unique one in many respects, but I have come to realize that I am a sinner first and foremost (like everyone) in great need of a Savior on a daily basis.

I found hope along life's journey often through the wonderful people I met, some of whom became great mentors. Caring people reached out a hand and lifted me up, never giving me a hand out. My marriage started 8/24/1968 and lasted a total of 19 years. For that I am very thankful.

Considering when we came home from our elopement I had a net worth of $10, I still feel grateful that I was able to earn well over $60,000 a year at age 23 thanks to mentors, a great work attitude, a wonderful employer, and a lot of long hours of diligent work, and through the grace of God.

You don't want all the details of all my life journey. I respectfully want to tell you how I came to discover "Ultimate Hope" so that you can too. Please consider:

Jesus to me is Hope with a capital H. I really am nothing with out my Lord Jesus, and I want to be sure to write that clearly and give Him all credit and glory for any and all successes I have had in my life to date. If I had it all to do over again, I would have preferred it was a more "traditional" life. You know what I mean? …after graduation from high school, go to college for 4-6 years, attain a good career position and work for the same company for 40+ years and then, retire. This kind of scenario is fading from reality for most everyone, it seems, so let's not cry over spilled milk. Remember, "God causes all things to work together for good…" Romans 8:28

> **The past is past, a canceled check. Learn from it.**
>
> **The present is ready cash, spend it very wisely.**
>
> **The future is a promissory note, will it be here at**
>
> **all or in the ways you prefer? You must hope better now!**

Yes, it is the mercy and grace of God, I know very strongly, that sustains me in the present moment so that I have any chance of cashing in on a future at all. I do believe in positive expectancy and have taught seminars for 30 years where I explored the **law of attraction** or how we attract to us good things or people or blessings in the future through a certain kind of thinking in the present... and the opposite can be true too!

I must cleanse myself of all misgivings, sins, and bad habits— starting with thoughts— before I can hope rightly for a great future. I have learned this lesson repeatedly. That is one reason I converted from the Protestant Church world to the Catholic Church right after I was about to be ordained a Protestant Minister because of an understanding about the seven Sacraments of the Church, specifically here I am thinking about the Sacrament of Reconciliation or Penance, or as commonly called... Confession.

Confession is a marvelous grace from God. You can find healing by confessing your sins direct to God. This is true. And, there is benefit in confessing your sins to others in a spirit of confidentiality. It is hard for me to believe some people actually seem to claim or believe they are not sinners. Who has deluded these people!? Denial is a big sin in itself. And, pride is the first sin of our ancestors, Adam and Eve, and at the root of all sin. Pride could keep you from being your best because you refuse to come to grips with your sins; so you may be doomed to repeat them in the future, maybe go to hell! There is HOPE!

Hope from our Triune God, as dispensed by the original Mother Church, the true and holy Roman Catholic Church (Roman because both Peter and Paul went to Rome, and Catholic which means universal) is so wonderful! With the successor of Peter— the Pope—as the visible head on earth now of the Church—you can find extreme and lasting Hope in the person of Jesus, due to a total cleansing of your sins by sacramental confession.

I am not making this up! It is true! Our God is True! I have experienced His total forgiveness and a NEW START repeatedly in the 17 years I have been Catholic, and I must say I have found an Ultimate Hope I never knew before as a very committed and devout Protestant Christian.

Please… don't knock it until you have tried it! And please realize that there are millions of uninformed sinful Catholics who do not obey the Church teachings so they are not a good source of Ultimate Truth. Go to a priest or better yet, the local Catholic Bishop, the local apostolic successor of Jesus through Peter, the first Pope. Hands have been laid on for ordination successively the Catholic Bishops in an unbroken string now since the Last Supper when Jesus ordained His first priests nearly 2000 years ago. Jesus gave Bishops, and then priests ordained by Bishops, the right to forgive sins on earth (John 20).

One week not long ago, I think I went to confession three in the same week. I had sin on my soul that was bothering me and I wanted to be clean as snow so that I could serve people with love and truth. I knew I needed the grace—unmerited favor—of God as one can experience in confession. Remember Jesus said to, "pray without ceasing".

One of the most important things we must always pray for is the forgiveness of our sins. In the "Our Father" prayer, Jesus clearly taught to pray, "and… forgive us our trespasses (or sins) as we forgive those who trespass against us". Never forget that forgiving others is a master key to getting your own self cleaned up, right, forgiven.

Fasting and Prayer

I remember one time in my first marriage, I was having a hard time being the husband I wanted to be for her mostly having to do with some challenges in my work. I had been to a Protestant church service where the minister spoke about the benefits of fasting and prayer, so I thought I needed to do more fasting: denial of myself to get clarity of mind, clarity of direction, answered prayer. I began to fast and did a total fast for three days (water only), and sure enough God answered my prayers and He gave me great hope, a strength to change and persevere.

Due to fasting, and prayer, I was given a plan to follow, and hope to follow it. Now, having been self employed most of the prior 32 years, I, like millions of others, have found some weeks are more challenging than others. There are many roads one can follow, and although many roads may lead to the same destination, <u>there is usually one best road</u>. You can discover your best path through fasting and prayer.

Most people know what prayer is and practice it, at least occasionally. Prayer in simple terms, is communication with God. And, as with any good communication, you must listen as much or more than you talk, if you want to "Win Friends and Influence People", as Dale Carnegie put it in his famous book. Who is more important to win as your best friend then our almighty and ever loving kind and gentle, willing to bless you, Lord Triune God!? There is only one true God, don't be fooled by counterfeits.

Talk to God more in prayer and you can do so better when you are more pleasing to Him, that makes sense, cleansed from your sins. So, you start your prayers as in the often recited "Our Father" prayer with Adoration and then a request for forgiveness of sins. The Holy Catholic Church teaches, by the way, that the only reason you need to go to confession is for forgiveness of "the seven capital (or deadly) sins". Other sins are called venial or more minor, and are taken care of at the beginning of a Catholic Mass in a certain rite. But for the BIG seven of pride, covetousness, lust, anger, gluttony, envy, and sloth, we go to confession, the Sacrament of Penance.

Now I don't want to turn this into an in-depth theology lesson. I want to give you my stories and how I have **found more hope so you can too**. I want to encourage you, in the love of Christ our Savior, to check out more carefully what the church teaches. Recently I taught what the Catholic Catechism—the official teaching of the Church—says to some adults at St. Michael Church in my home city, and I realized I the teacher was benefiting the most. I realized I can pray better, be better! You too? Yes!

And, truly I have found fasting to be a great benefit to my connecting with God so that I can not only hear my prayers being answered (or what God has to say to me). I can get strengthened to deny my selfishness and weak flesh for a more victorious future with a life of hope.

Fasting is encouraged by Mother Church during Lent (40 days leading up to Easter) especially, and during Advent (weeks before Christmas) too. Unfortunately due to the so-called Protestant reformation primarily started by Martin Luther, (an unrepentant Catholic priest) many start-up churches threw the baby out with the bath water, so to speak. The Bible—which was codified by the Catholic Church and exists only because of the Catholic Church—has always taught the value of fasting and prayer.

Fasting in particular in the Old Testament, was a way to loose the bonds of bad habits or sinfulness. Reconnect with God. Rather than quote a lot of verses as proof texts, which I could easily do throughout my writings in this book, I assert statements as fact or truth, largely because millions understand these statements as truth and need no proof text, only friendly reminders or challenges.

Fasting in the New Testament is shown most vividly in the life of Jesus, with one classic example of how He, after his baptism in the Jordan River by John the Baptizer, went into the dessert where he fasted and prayed for 40 days (and of course 40 nights too). Wow! Can you imagine going with out food for 40 days? I suppose He had water but the scripture does not clearly say that He did. He was preparing for the greatest three years of work that ever took place on earth!!! Want to prepare for some great work?

> **Fast… and pray. Get right and serious with God. You will find the right kind of hope and a lot of it as a result. I guarantee it!**

When starting a fast, you may want to see your doctor first and/ or get some spiritual advice or direction from a trusted minister. But, realize regardless of what others say, going with out a meal or two or more, will help you much more than hurt you (in most cases), especially if you connect it with better prayers.

To say, "I have not sinned." Or, "I am not a sinner." … this may be the worst sin of all. "This attitude could be the sin that keeps a person from going to heaven", I heard a priest recently say. Why? Because in believing "I am not a sinner!" this person is claiming he or she does not need God; or in reality, "I am God!"—worse yet!

> **We all need God! The most unbelieving atheist or agnostic person needs God! God have mercy on all unbelievers! Please create in them a heart that can accept God's Truh. I pray, we imperfect people will not distract them from Perfection.**

Journeys

Most people like to go on exciting journeys. One such journey in my history was our trip to the Holy land, Israel's Jerusalem and the holy cities and locations where Jesus appeared, just after my marriage to Lorna Millan, my second (and current and last!) wife. We had just been blessed by a Sacramental Church Marriage on 11/23/91 and asked at our reception for "prayer requests to be taken to the Church of the Nativity in Bethlehem tomorrow". One of our stops on that 10 day honeymoon was to the Jordan River where reportedly (the very spot!) Jesus was baptized.

We approached this location after a trip north of Jerusalem to Nazareth—"He will be called a Nazarene"—and when going south on the road along the Jordan River, before coming to the ancient city of Jericho, we encountered something I have only seen once in my life.

Have you ever seen a double rainbow? Do you know the story of the "bow" placed in the sky by God after 40 days and 40 nights of rain that destroyed all living things on earth except those in the ark with Noah? These kinds of true—let's not consider it a myth—stories in the scripture can provide great hope! Anyway, as Lorna and I rode in the small touring bus, we were amazed by the sign God was giving us, a rainbow for each of us to signify His binding and promised love for our marriage. Wow!

God is so good, so loving, and He provides signs all the time to show us the way to go in our lives, if we are well connected to Him. Get connected and stay connected!

Ultimate hope is Jesus and His promise of eternal life fulfilled once we depart this life. Your heavenly destiny God intends to be a place of ultimate beauty, serenity, peace, lasting reward and life eternal with God and all the holy angels and saints. Hope Fulfilled!

Paradise in heaven is better than the best vacation spot on earth—it is the ultimate resting place where praising God comes naturally and is easy coming from a purified heart totally grace filled of unending gratitude.

> **May all your purified hopes be fulfilled! May our Perfect God bless you, and give you His peace, more success in this life, and life eternal—Ultimate Hope!**

Hopeful and Inspiring Co-authors and Contributors information In alphabetical order

Greg Bennick is an award-winning professional keynote entertainer and speaker. He has spoken before corporate and other specialized audiences at conferences, seminars, and universities in over a dozen countries on four continents. He focuses on group dynamics and communication skills, with an emphasis on how emotional intelligence plays a role in personal and collective development. And, he's funny. He writes, entirely unedited, his own bio information for books to which he contributes. He can be reached through his website at www.gregbennick.com.

Jo Ann Bennett-Boltinghouse: A Self-Esteem Advocate, Jo Ann's mission in life is "to help people be better at what they do, no matter what that may be." She is an educator, trainer, speaker and a grandmother. She resides in Iowa with her husband, Earl and YolandaBaby. When Jo Ann isn't teaching or writing, she can be found curled up with a great book and a bowl of popcorn, enjoying world-wide travel with family and friends or creating new ideas for interacting with her grandchildren. boltingh@ harlannet.com

Vitalia Bryn-Pundyk, M.Ed., ACG/CL: As an active member of the National Speakers Association and Toastmasters International, Vitalia Bryn-Pundyk is an award-winning speaker and is recognized as an ACG (Advanced Communicator Gold) and a CL (Competent Leader). Vitalia graduated from the University of Minnesota with a M.Ed. in Second Languages and Cultures with a minor in Theatre, and completed the "Dale

Carnegie" and "Leadership Training for Managers" courses at the Dale Carnegie Institute, where she received the "Most Outstanding Performance" and "Human Relations" awards. Vitalia's leadership experience includes both the small business and corporate world. She is the founder and director of "La Fiesta School of Spanish," a former senior trainer and business development strategist with "Summit Group International," and the President and CEO of "Vitalia Success Seminars," offering high–impact motivational leadership training and mentoring courses that enhance communication effectiveness and people management skills. To learn more about Vitalia's motivational programs and how you can hire her for your next small business or corporate event, go to **www.vitaliasuccessseminar.com.** Be sure to check out her monthly newsletter "Maximize Your Potential!" for additional success strategy tips!

Lisa M. Buldo: Lisa is a graduate of the Institute for Integrative Nutrition which is accredited by the American Association of Drugless Practitioners. She is also the Founder and Executive Director of "Natural Whole Health, L.L.C.," a Nutrition and Lifestyle Coaching Company located in Bergen County, New Jersey. As a Certified Holistic Health Counselor and Certified Biblical Health Coach, Lisa looks at the "whole person," which means physically, as well as emotionally and spiritually. Lisa's journey into health and wellness was a natural one due to the fact that Lisa suffered with severe allergies and asthma most of her life. She battled acne for 15 years and has suffered with digestive issues. All of these things led Lisa wholeheartedly to her passion for health and nutrition, and accordingly, Lisa has been a researcher of health and nutrition for the last 10 years. lisa@lisabuldo.com

Liz Cosline is an author of four books and certified Life Ownership Coach. She is now in the process of writing her fifth book. She started a website where she shares poetry, thoughts, her books, and business articles. Liz has been in business management for over 23 years. Liz has been on several radio programs and has reviews by, Midwest Review, Coffee Time Romace, The New Book review, and many others.   http:songofoneunexpectedlife.info

Chic Dambach is President and CEO of the Alliance for Peacebuilding, a coalition of 50 organizations working together to build sustainable peace and security worldwide. From 1992 through 1999, he was President of the National Peace Corps Association. Chic was part of a team of returned Peace Corps Volunteers who worked informally with the leaders of Eritrea and Ethiopia to help end their border war. The team has also worked with rebel leaders and the government of the Congo to help them form a coalition government leading to elections and end the civil war. He has been a featured speaker at US Department of State sponsored national and regional Town Meetings, and he lectures frequently at colleges and universities. Chic was an official U.S. delegate to the United Nations World Food Conference in Rome in 2000. He is chairman of the Coalition for American Leadership Abroad, and he serves on the board of the J. William and Harriet Fulbright Center as well as the Global Partnership to Prevent Armed Conflict. He was an official in the 1988, 1992 and 1996 Olympic Games, and he was a Peace Corps Volunteer in Colombia from 1967 through 1969. chic@dambach.org

NOTE: These contributors can be located for scheduling them to speak at the website: www.TerrificSpeakers.com ; for a short cut go to TOPICS from the tool bar, use the Google search box, type in their name staying on website.

Amy Drake is a Columbus, Ohio based writer who has worked in communications for a large corporation. Amy was a recipient of a 2008 Silver Quill Award of Excellence for on-line writing from the International Association of Business Communicators. She holds a B.A. from Ohio Dominican University and is currently pursuing a master's degree from ODU, having earned a place on the National Dean's List. Amy studied history and creative writing in summer programs at the University of Cambridge, UK and completed a master's course in literature at Reed Hall, Paris, France. She has written for Nationwide's web sites and on-line newsletters, and other publications including <u>Pageantry, Guitar Digest, Now It's Dark Magazine,</u> The Columbus Blues Alliance "Bluespaper," and <u>Wellpoint</u>. Amy has been a title holder in the Beauties of America Pageant and has appeared on stage in the OperaColumbus productions of <u>Madame Butterfly</u> and <u>Carmen</u> and in the film <u>Angie</u>. She currently serves on the Board of the English Speaking Union, reads for VOICECORPS and is an active member of the International Association for Business Communicators. McGeeAmy110@aol.com

Jerry Gay is a Pulitzer Prize winning photojournalist and exceptional public speaker who presents impassioned visuals and philosophical insights to reflect moments of universal importance. He has worked with major newspapers: Los Angeles Times, Newsday and Seattle Times, as well as radio and multi-media corporations. Recently, he drove over 60,000 miles across every state to study and document insightful moments of societal transformation. Jerry Gay has become the visual master of inspirational communication that reflects America's evolvement into spiritual consciousness. jerry@jerrygay.com

Katharine Giovanni: A highly sought-after expert on the concierge industry, Katharine has both been interviewed by and appeared on dozens of newspapers, magazines, radio and television shows from around the country. A dynamic public speaker and a member of the National Speakers Association, Katharine has appeared at seminars and conferences around the county. She is an acclaimed author as well. Her titles include ***The Concierge Manual, Going Above and Beyond*** and her inspirational book

God is that you? She can be reached through her website at www. triangleconcierge.com and www.katharinegiovanni.com

Mark Gorkin, MSW, LICSW, "The Stress Doc" ™, a Licensed Clinical Social Worker, is an acclaimed keynote and kickoff speaker and "Motivational Humorist" known for his interactive, inspiring and *FUN* speaking and workshop programs. In addition, the "Doc" is a team building and organizational development consultant for a variety of govt. agencies, corporations and non-profits and is AOL's "Online Psychohumorist" ™. Mark is an Adjunct Professor, No. VA (NOVA) Community College and currently he is leading "Stress, Team Building and Humor" programs for the 1st Cavalry and 4th Infantry Divisions, Ft. Hood, Texas. For more info on the Doc's "Practice Safe Stress" programs or to receive his free e-newsletter, email **stressdoc@aol. com** or call **301-946-0865**.

Helene B. Leonetti, MD has journeyed from nurse to doctor, to author, to researcher, to reiki master, and humbly finds herself back to the beginning, and as I think the great writer, TS Elliott says, she is seeing the place for the first time. She is manifesting her life's mission by affirming what she has found: that loving oneself unconditionally and with great compassion is the prerequisite to a peace-filled and divinely orchestrated life. Although I am board certified in Holistic Medicine as well as OB-GYN, a well-trained herbalist by master herbalist, David Winston, acknowledged worldwide for my research with natural transdermal progesterone, and have fifteen years helping women manage their hormone imbalance with bio-identical hormones, I have come to one powerful realization: that is until we magnificent goddesses love and honor ourselves before serving our families and the world—we cannot be healthy. Helene_B.Leonetti@lvh.com

Lorna M. Lisk, MS Lorna has ministered to thousands in the USA, Europe, Asia and Latin and North America, including many diocesan Catholic Charismatic Renewal groups in the cities of London, Dublin, Rome and Belize. She has conducted healing services for parishioners after Masses for Charismatic, Rosary and Cursillo groups. Lorna is the author of *Boost Your Prayer Power*. She and her husband give talks on this topic also. She is the founder-president of 16 year old Worldwide United Prayer for Christ, a worldwide prayer network with millions of prayer partners which has been promoted in 50 countries on 6 continents. She was named Catholic Woman of the Year for 2002 in the 23 county diocese of Columbus, Ohio. Having been in the Catholic charismatic renewal for the past 27 years, she also is founder-coordinator of several Rosary groups in a few states and is a member of Cursillo. Having been listed in the World Who's Who of Women, she has degrees in B.S. Chemical Engineering and M.S. Chemistry. Pope John Paul II gave her his apostolic blessings. Their healing and evangelism ministry and Worldwide United Prayer for Christ are among ministries listed in latest National Catholic Charismatic Renewal Leadership Directory. Lorna and Thom have five married children with 11 grandchildren. speak@terrificspeaker.com

Dr. Thomas (Thom) A. Lisk, BA, LHD, CSE is a proven leader of leaders, as well as leadership lecturer, keynote speaker, consultant and facilitator of leadership topics for both profit and non-profit entities: empowerment, strategic planning, personal development formation, organizational development, sales, marketing, and ethics for profit and non-profit entities. Thom has a personal message about overcoming many adversities (not just stress or change) including near death to persevere and experience success. His degrees include Bachelors in Arts, double major, Leadership Communications from Capital University, graduating magna cum laude. He has a doctorate degree in Humane Letters (L.H.D.) from Southern California Seminary, and has an earned certification (CSE) accrediting him an ethical sales and marketing leader from Sales & Marketing Executives International. Thom has completed additional formal university education (Masters Level) in business, psychology, human resource management, meeting planning, and theology. Thom-Terrific is the author of five books, the first of which was co-authored/published in 1981 — *Those Marvelous Mentors*. Preceding Noble Leadership© (2002), Thom wrote the Bible for all salespeople, *Become #1 in Selling* published first in 1996. In 2008 Penquin/USA -- NY, NY worldwide publisher -- released Lisk's book, *The Complete Idiot's Guide to Success as a Professional Speaker*. Lisk is President of Professional Speakers Bureau Int'l, a worldwide association of speakers that serves as a bureau booking hundreds of different speakers (500 are featured on the website with 5000 speakers on file). Go-to: www.TerrificSpeakers.com Thom Lisk is the recipient of the prestigious *Norman Vincent Peale Lifetime Achievement Award in Speaking*. Lisk has served as President of for-profit companies including PSBI, Direct Resource Institute, The Thom Lisk Group, as well as President of non-profits including The Independent Consultants Association, The Christian Business Management Association, The Catholic Men's Ministry, Diocese of Columbus. Lisk clients have included the Fortune 500 and national and state associations of all types. Lisk is the recipient of the prestigious Paul Harris Fellowship Award (named after Founder) from Rotary International. Lisk served as a Trustee in several organizations including his civic association, United Way, etc. And as Chairperson for numerous events Lisk is an expert meetings leader and pro speaker and expert to help you evaluate all speakers: Contact Lisk: **ThomLisk@TerrificSpeakers.com**

Dr. Susan Murphy: Dr. Susan Murphy is a business and organizational consultant whose background includes over 25 years of national and international experience with over 300 organizations including many Fortune 500 companies. Her clients include the U.S. Air Force, the Jet Propulsion Lab (JPL), Stanford University and the American Hospital Association. Susan has an extensive background, which combines the three worlds of corporate leadership, academia and management consulting. She has been an Executive in two Fortune 500 Corporations, has served on the faculty at the University of San Francisco, Graduate School, and has performed corporate-wide international management consulting for 20 years to a variety of industries. She specializes in Leadership and Team Development, Gender Differences, Change Management, Performance Management, and Customer Service. Susan has written four books. drsmurphy@consult4business.com

Michael A. Schadek is the creator of "2 Acts of Kindness" and coaches individuals and organizations to help change the world and their lives—two acts at a time. A graduate of the University of Notre Dame and Cleveland-Marshall College of Law, Mr. Schadek has enjoyed success as an attorney and businessman. Working with Archbishop Desmond Tutu in Cape Town, South Africa inspired his passion to help change the world. Mr. Schadek resides in Columbus, Ohio with his wife and two sons. His daughter is in Heaven. For more information, go to www.2aok.com

Dr. Charles D. Schmitz and Dr. Elizabeth A. Schmitz: As America's #1 Love and Marriage Experts and multiple award-winning authors, Dr. Charles D. Schmitz and Dr. Elizabeth A. Schmitz help audiences around the world answer questions about love, marriage and relationships. Their distinguished careers include over 65 awards, 350 books, articles and manuscripts, 1000 speeches, and frequent media appearances. With 26 years of research on relationships and successful marriage on five continents of the world and their own 42-year marriage, the Doctors know what makes relationships work. To learn more about love and marriage visit the Doctors at: www.GoldenAnniversaries.com

Dr. Brenda Shoshanna, psychologist, long term practitioner of both Zen and Judaism, is the author of award winning Jewish Dharma (A Guide to the Practice of Judaism and Zen), Perseus

Books, www.jewishdharma.com. Radio show host of It's A New Day with Dr Shoshanna, www.progressiveradionetwork.com, Wed. 2-3, and regular guest on radio and TV, she has offered over 500 talks, workshops on all aspects of personal and spiritual growth and developing authentic peace of mind. Some of her other books include The Anger Diet, (30 Days to Stress Free Living), Zen and the Art of Falling in Love and many others. http://www.jewishdharma.com. Contact her at: topspeaker@yahoo.com, (212) 288-0028. www.brendashoshanna.com

Kathy Slamp: Raised in a pastor's home, Kathy has also been a pastor's wife for over 35 years. Her speaking takes her from coast to coast where she speaks to groups of all sizes and many different denominations. Her down-to-earth sincerity and sense of humor endear her to audiences wherever she goes. Kathy's spiritual depth and life experiences make her someone with whom people easily relate. She was selected to be in the 2007 Who's Who of American women. Kathy taught public school for many years at all levels (kindergarten--college) and served as a high school assistant principal. She is married to Dr. David A. Slamp who is a pastor in Oregon. They have two grown children and two grandsons. Through her speaking and writing, Kathy inspires and challenges her audiences to grasp the basic and vital Biblical concept: We are all chosen to carry this amazing treasure: ***Christ in you is the hope of glory.*** As Christians in this world, God chooses to use each and everyone of us as His vessels! vesselmin@yahoo.com

Angela Gracia Smith is the "adding health to life ambassador" ™. For over twenty years, Angela has been facilitating programs and writing educational materials in English and Spanish. Her Healthy Equations™ seminars and interactive displays are hands-on and filled with practical ways to enjoy adding the wealth of great health each day. Gain health today, visit www.angelagsmith.com.

Carol Stevens, founder and President of Your Training Solutions, L.P., has an extensive background in strategic consulting, curriculum development and training delivery. Her expertise in managing people and projects brings an invaluable perspective to her sessions. Carol knows the slight edge difference that HOPE creates, and the positive impact that HOPE and a contagiously positive attitude can make in organizations. She takes great pride in equipping leaders to enhance their team's productivity and their personal leadership effectiveness through dynamic, engaging presentations. Learn more about Carol at www.yourtrainingsolutions.com.

Arlene R. Taylor PhD, one of the world's leading speakers on brain function, is sometimes referred to as the *brain guru*. She specializes in simplifying this complex topic of brain function—unleashing one's potential to thrive. Whether through keynote addresses, seminars, consulting, coaching, television and radio, or her books, CDs, and DVDs, success stories pour in from the four corners of the world. Dr. Taylor is founder and president of Realizations Inc, a non-profit corporation involved with brain-function research and with providing related educational resources. TaylorAR@shpo.ah.org

Despite severe medical setbacks and against insurmountable odds, **DR. STEVEN VLADEM** has made amazing accomplishments, first as an outstanding and innovative educator and computer specialist, and later, he was recognized for the work he has done in setting up transplant centers all over the world, which will result in saving millions of lives. Dr. Vladem is also a motivational speaker and role model, who has inspired many individuals who are physically challenged. Dr. Vladem has been a strong advocate to prevent intolerance and discrimination against handicapped individuals. Dr. Vladem has shown a great deal of courage in rising above a devastating experience and triumphing above adversity to help others. Dr. Vladem's numerous accomplishments and achievements are documented in many national and international Who's Who biographical reference works, including Marquis Who's Who in America and Marquis Who's Who in the World. He has received a large number of prestigious national and international awards from a wide variety of organizations, and he has received many knighthoods for his service to mankind. Dr. Vladem's eagerly awaited autobiography will be published soon. Three motion pictures about his life experiences are being planned. stevevladem@yahoo.com

Diane F. Wyzga, RN, JD: Imagine this: a former United States Navy nurse, business woman, and litigator goes back to her roots and learns the value of stories and storytelling to persuade, guide and inspire. Today she takes those skills on the road as Lightning Rod Communications to train lawyers and corporate leaders and management staff to identify, shape and effectively deliver their stories using language with power, passion and precision. Her clients effectively incorporate storytelling techniques and principles in their professional and personal communication by learning to translate compelling images into desired action. diane@lightrod.net

Coach Z Rich Zvosec: Coach Z is a college basketball analyst for ESPN, motivational speaker, published author and actor. His first book is titled "Birds, Dogs and Kangaroos: Life on the Back Roads of College Basketball." In 2005 he became one of only 35 active college basketball coaches to be selected Coach of the Year in two different Division I conferences at separate schools. That year he was selected the Mid-Continent Conference, CBS Sportsline and College Insider.com Coach of the Year for his team's performance at UMKC. He has a reputation as a rebuilder of programs and his speaking programs deal with "turning adversity into advantage." Also, you will learn how to Drink, Swear, Steal and Lie your way to success. Finally, learn about the "backpack of life" at www.CoachZLive.com.

More information about all people in this book and other authors and speakers go-to: www.TerrificSpeakers.com. For scheduling as a speaker the contributors above use links on this website or phone 614-841-1776. Thank you.

Dr. Lisk will make a donation to the *Legacy of Hope Society* and Habitat for Humanity from profits from the sale of this book. Help us leave a legacy of hope!

BUY A SHARE OF THE FUTURE IN YOUR COMMUNITY

These certificates make great holiday, graduation and birthday gifts that can be personalized with the recipient's name. The cost of one S.H.A.R.E. or one square foot is $54.17. The personalized certificate is suitable for framing and will state the number of shares purchased and the amount of each share, as well as the recipient's name. The home that you participate in "building" will last for many years and will continue to grow in value.

Here is a sample SHARE certificate:

YES, I WOULD LIKE TO HELP!

I support the work that Habitat for Humanity does and I want to be part of the excitement! As a donor, I will receive periodic updates on your construction activities but, more importantly, I know my gift will help a family in our community realize the dream of homeownership. **I would like to SHARE in your efforts against substandard housing in my community!** *(Please print below)*

PLEASE SEND ME _____ SHARES at $54.17 EACH = $ $_____

In Honor Of: _____

Occasion: (Circle One) HOLIDAY BIRTHDAY ANNIVERSARY

OTHER: _____

Address of Recipient: _____

Gift From: _____ *Donor Address:* _____

Donor Email: _____

I AM ENCLOSING A CHECK FOR $ $_____ PAYABLE TO HABITAT FOR HUMANITY OR PLEASE CHARGE MY VISA OR MASTERCARD *(CIRCLE ONE)*

Card Number _____ Expiration Date: _____

Name as it appears on Credit Card _____ Charge Amount $ _____

Signature _____

Billing Address _____

Telephone # Day _____ Eve _____

PLEASE NOTE: Your contribution is tax-deductible to the fullest extent allowed by law.
Habitat for Humanity • P.O. Box 1443 • Newport News, VA 23601 • 757-596-5553
www.HelpHabitatforHumanity.org